THE
Accountability
ADVANTAGE

Sam Silverstein

THE
Accountability
ADVANTAGE

Design a sustainable,
high-performance culture to
build stronger businesses,
communities, and people

Published and distributed by:
SOUND WISDOM
P.O. Box 310
Shippensburg, PA 17257-0310
717-530-2122

info@soundwisdom.com

www.soundwisdom.com

ISBN 13 TP: 978-1-64095-378-9

ISBN 13 eBook: 978-1-64095-379-6

For Worldwide Distribution, Printed in the U.S.A.

1 2 3 4 5 6 7 8 / 26 25 24 23 22

Contents

I

Foundational
PRINCIPLES

Chapter 1

The Pain in the Butt

ONE MORNING, A FEW YEARS AGO, I woke up and discovered I was experiencing immense and acute discomfort in the region of my gluteus maximus. That's right, I had a major pain in my butt.

I should give you a little background here. For the past week, that pain in my butt had been growing steadily. Each time I had noticed it, I had dismissed it. *No problem*, I thought. *It will go away on its own. That's what happens with muscle pains.* Which is what I had convinced myself this was: muscle pain.

Well, for a week this so-called "muscle pain" had refused to go away. It kept intensifying. One day, I decided I had better back off on my running routine. So I did not run as many miles, hoping that would make things better. It did not. As the week wore on, I went from not running as many miles to not running at all. The pain just kept getting worse, no matter what I did. I kept trying to struggle through it. I devoted three days to pretending I could tough it out. Then four. Then five. Finally, on a Sunday morning at 5:30 A.M., I woke up in so much pain that I told my wife Renee, "I can't do this anymore. We have to go to the hospital."

Renee drove me to the emergency room. When they asked me how bad the pain was, on a scale of 1 to 10, I said, "Fifteen!" I meant it. I was in bad shape.

I had an MRI, which revealed that the problem was not muscle fatigue, as I had thought. It looked to the doctors like a disc issue, and a serious one. I would have to see a specialist to get a formal diagnosis—someone who could evaluate the MRI I had just completed. But there were no neurosurgeons available to see me that morning. They sent me home with some pain medication.

The pain pills did very little for me. I could not sit down for any length of time without feeling like I was going through a torture chamber. A visit to a pain specialist brought me back to a basic level of functionality—meaning I was no longer in level 15 agony. I was down to about a 5 or a 6. So I could sit down, grit my teeth, and bear the pain for just long enough to take a flight from St. Louis to Reno, Nevada, to give a speech I had been booked for that week. (For some reason, standing up was much less of a problem than sitting down.) Once I made it back home, it became more obvious than ever that just masking the pain was not the solution I was looking for. This was no way to live. I knew I had to see a back specialist if I wanted to get to the bottom of this—and get something resembling a normal life back.

With Renee's help and support, and the help and support of Dr. Rob Kramer, a friend of a friend of ours, I was able to get an appointment with a neurosurgeon who was able to confirm what the ER doctors had found. This was a disc problem, and fixing it meant making some lifestyle changes that would not necessarily be comfortable or familiar. There would be a special exercise routine I would need to follow. Also, I would have to stop running marathons and run shorter distances… or even replace running altogether with other forms of exercise.

Now, this is a book about organizational culture. So perhaps you are wondering: Why am I telling you all this? Because leaders and organizations wake up to discover they have a major pain in the butt, too! Often, in fact, they have more than one.

The Accountability Advantage™ process cures all organizational pains in the butt.

> The Accountability Advantage™ process cures all organizational pains in the butt.

SOME KEY TAKEAWAYS

Let me pause here and share some important takeaways—ones I believe are relevant not just to the emergency room, but to your organization:

> I thought I knew what was causing my pain in the butt. I was wrong. The specialist I ended up working with was 1,000 percent better at diagnosing the problem than I was. It turned out that the cause was not at all what I had imagined.
>
> Takeaway: We sometimes need help from an expert to figure out what is causing the pain and how best to deal with and resolve that pain.

Initially, I thought my pain in the butt was not serious. I was wrong about that, too. As a result, I took actions that made the problem worse.

Takeaway: When we ignore symptoms or try to fix the situation without a professional diagnosis, we run the risk of worsening the problem.

When I reached the point of agony, what I was most interested in was making the pain go away. I really wanted the doctor to prescribe a vial of magic pills that would accomplish that goal. A pain pill, however, was not all that I needed.

Takeaway: It is natural enough for us to focus on the pain we are feeling...but we need to understand that **the pain is a symptom of what we are going through, not the root cause.** We do not want to simply mask the symptoms and stop there. If we do, the problem returns and is even more difficult to solve.

The pain I was feeling expressed itself in the form of any number of specific challenges that were also (as it were) a pain in the butt for me. For instance, I was having trouble getting out of bed. That was a pain in the butt. I could not drive, and I could not sit in an airplane seat. That was a pain in the butt. If I had tried to deliver a speech in front of a group while I was at a level 15 on the pain scale, it would not have been pretty. I am a professional speaker, so not being able to do what I do best was definitely a pain in the butt. However, none of those specific challenges I faced were the **root cause** of the big problem I was facing.

Takeaway: Challenges in execution and performance must not be confused with the root causes that create those challenges.

When I followed my neurosurgeon's advice over a period of weeks, I recovered. My pain in the butt disappeared. I could get out of bed on my own. I could drive again. I could sit in an airplane seat again. I could deliver programs and keynote speeches again.

Takeaway: When you fix the root problem, the related pains in the butt vanish.

This experience was awful. I did not want the pain to ever come back. That meant I had to make a long-term commitment to the therapy regimen that the back specialist shared with me. I could not stop doing what I needed to do after a week or so of following his advice. I had to make some long-term changes. And I had to be committed to stepping the new regimen out over time.

Takeaway: If you maintain the new routine, you keep the old problems from resurfacing...and you keep the pain from coming back.

This story is not really about me. It is about you and your organization. It is an analogue for the *challenges organizations experience when the working culture has a serious problem.*

Do leaders ever imagine that a pain in the butt will go away on its own...ignore or minimize the symptoms...and thereby turn a minor pain in the butt into a major one? I think you know the answer.

Do leaders ever misdiagnose the cause of a major pain in the butt? You bet they do.

Do they ever reach for a "pain pill" that will mask the symptoms and imagine they have solved the problem? I have seen it happen more times than I can count.

Do they ever try to fix challenges in execution and performance without addressing the root cause of those challenges? Yes!

Do they ever start down the right track, then fall back into old habits and routines that make it inevitable that they and their organizations will experience a major pain in the butt all over again? You know they do.

Do they ever accept what seems like a minor pain in the butt because they are making money? Yes—and if they made the effort necessary to properly diagnose and eliminate the pain in the butt, the profits would be far greater!

WHAT IS YOUR MAJOR PAIN IN THE BUTT?

So what does your organization's major "pain in the butt" feel like? Is it underperformance in any of the following areas?

Most organizations will be thrilled to make dramatic improvements in one of these areas. And if they were able to make dramatic improvements in two or three of these areas, they would be elated.

But what would happen if you were somehow able to transform your organizational, Monday-morning "pain in the butt" into a sustainable competitive advantage…in *all eleven areas*?

Is that even possible? What would it look like?

Glad you asked. It would look like this:

> Transforming a pain in the butt in the area of **Leadership** into a sustainable competitive advantage means making your organization a well-oiled machine.
>
> It means people at all levels of the organization consistently make the best decisions possible at that level—on their own—and ask for help in making decisions only in rare or extraordinary situations. It means your people make good decisions quickly and move forward expeditiously. It means your people have the resources and the support they need to get the job done.

Transforming a pain in the butt in the area of **Communication** into a sustainable competitive advantage means your people know what they need to know, when they need to know it.

It means information flows freely through the organization, not just within a given team but between teams. It means siloed communication does not exist in your organization. It means nothing is held back for petty or immature or short-sighted reasons. It means no backbiting and no gossiping. It means everything important is shared openly and honestly, and information is virtually always received in the way that it was intended.

Transforming a pain in the butt in the area of **Teamwork** into a sustainable competitive advantage means your people trust each other and know they can count on each other.

People are ready, willing, and able to help each other, and they are ready, willing, and able to ask for help when they need it. They are not worried about what people think about them, because they know that they are all in this together.

Transforming a pain in the butt in the area of the *Customer Experience* into a sustainable competitive advantage means you have great word of mouth in the marketplace.

It means your customers feel valued. You have a strong base of happy customers who have a high statistical likelihood of becoming repeat customers, and there is no shortage of quality referrals. Ever.

Transforming a pain in the butt in the area of *Change* into a sustainable competitive advantage means your organization is flexible, adaptable, and resourceful, no matter what is happening in the marketplace.

It means there is a willingness to change because people trust leadership and trust each other. When change is important and the need for change is communicated across teams, people assume that leadership is making decisions that are in their best interest. As a result, they are positioned to accept the change and implement the change more quickly—which means the organization reaps the benefits of that change quickly. Change simply becomes a decision.

Transforming a pain in the butt in the area of **Creativity and Innovation** into a sustainable competitive advantage means everyone is valued for their opinion.

Everyone is willing to share their opinion, which means that people who are involved or affected by a given process and who have insights that will help you to improve that process share their ideas when it counts. It means people at all levels feel comfortable sharing new ideas. And it means that disruptive technology has a greater likelihood of being discovered and implemented—and improving your position in the marketplace.

Transforming a pain in the butt in the area of **Safety** into a sustainable competitive advantage means your people are free to focus on what is really important.

Of course, this transformation means that everyone is physically safe. But it also means that people feel **emotionally** safe—safe to be who they are, safe to disagree with leadership, and safe to think freely. In a high-performance culture, it is safe to be different. Team members know they are not being judged, and they know that bias has no place in the organization.

Transforming a pain in the butt in the area of **Attraction and Retention** into a sustainable competitive advantage means your organization is able to attract and hold on to the best people, even when unemployment is low.

Because you are a "destination employer," you have a long line of qualified people applying for every opening. People know about and want to be associated with your organization because they want to work in a safe environment, one where they are valued, heard, and always considered to be part of the solution, not part of the problem.

Transforming a pain in the butt in the area of **Engagement** into a sustainable competitive advantage means people are fully aligned with the mission.

It means people enjoy working for your organization and enjoy working with each other, and it means they apply themselves to everything they do. It means team members are driven by a desire to do their best.

Transforming a pain in the butt in the area of *Productivity* into a sustainable competitive advantage means your return on investment improves.

Your people are getting more done, not just on behalf of the organization and your clients, but on behalf of **each other**—which strengthens those relationships internally. When engagement goes up, productivity goes up.

Transforming a pain in the butt in the area of *Profitability* into a sustainable competitive advantage means your bottom line is robust in both good times and bad.

You take better care of all your stakeholders, not just your employees and your investors. You attain your financial goals **and** make a positive impact on the community in which you do business. The competitive advantages listed above, which you have created in the good times, are significant strategic resources for you in more difficult times.

Many leaders look at me with deep skepticism when I tell them that it is possible to make these kinds of advances in all of these areas. They seem to think what I am describing is impossible. I am here to tell you that it is not. Excellence in all of these areas flows from one central optimization—the optimization of creating and protecting a *sustainable high-performance culture that people want to be a part of.*

> This book is about creating and protecting a sustainable high-performance culture that people want to be a part of.

Let me be very clear about something that a lot of people miss: you can hit your numbers and still *not* be creating a sustainable high-performance culture that people want to be a part of. That is exactly what many leaders do. When they do that, they put their organizations at risk!

It is true. You can make a lot of money, get good publicity, and rank high in your industry *without* creating and protecting the kind of working culture I am talking about. But you cannot do any of that in a way that increases your competitive edge and ensures your organization's success during good times and bad if you are experiencing multiple pains in the butt, which many organizations are.

To make the competition irrelevant and set up the kind of operational success that endures no matter what else is happening in the economy, you need to fix the *one* thing that is the predictable common denominator for all organizations in all eleven of those organizational pains in the butt we just examined.

Maybe you already know what that one thing is, and maybe you are already on the path to healing your organization. If that is the case, this book is going to help you maintain that trajectory and get where you need to go more quickly.

On the other hand, if you *do not* know what the cure for your pain in the butt is and you want to find out so you can heal your organization and keep it healed, this book will help you do that.

So keep reading. Whichever of those two groups you happen to fall into, it is important that you read this book as part of your daily routine. Read as much or as little as you like, but keep moving forward and read something from it once a day. Read it from beginning to end before you try to implement anything. Then *share* this book with the people in your organization as you implement the steps outlined in the chapters that follow.

> Read this book as part of your daily routine. Read as much or as little as you like, but keep moving forward and read something from it at least once a day. Read it from beginning to end before you try to implement anything. Then *share* this book with the people in your organization as you implement the steps outlined in the chapters that follow.

Ultimately, this book is for everyone. Why? Because it takes everyone in the organization to build an organization that people love.

> "Customers will never love a company until the employees love it first." —Simon Sinek

So, start the next chapter. And by that I mean the next chapter in this book...the next chapter for your organization...and the next chapter in your life.

Chapter 2

Culture by Design, Culture by Default

ARE YOU CURIOUS, but at the same time a little dubious, about what we've discussed so far? Be honest.

Do you feel at all skeptical that your organization really can attract and retain the very best people, all the time, so you always have a deep reservoir of both active talent and aspiring talent to choose from?

Do you wonder whether it is really possible for you to create a niche in your market that is literally beyond the reach of the competition?

Do you doubt that you really can secure deep levels of customer loyalty, posting retention and referral numbers that your competitors only dream of?

Perhaps most important of all, are you feeling some uncertainty that you, personally, really can make any of this happen in your world? Are you skeptical that all of this can happen from the inside, starting with you, based on the working culture *you* choose to create and defend at your organization?

If you are feeling any of those things right now, you should know that you are not alone. Many of the leaders we talk to about this subject are curious…and a bit dubious at first. They say things like…

"We tried something like this, and it didn't deliver the kind of results you're talking about."

If it did not deliver those results, then rest assured that this is *not* what you tried. Or it is not what you were committed to.

"We are too small for this. We handle organizational culture issues at a granular level."

If you are consistently experiencing even *one* of the pains in the butt that we looked at in the previous chapter, then it is time for a reality check. Your "granular approach" is not creating a positive, powerful, sustainable working culture, regardless of the size of your organization. In these pages, you will find powerful ideas for strategies that do work. Organizational culture always starts with the very first team member.

"We're too big for this. We have so many offices and so many interlocking pieces of the puzzle that it's really not possible to establish a cohesive working culture across all of those teams."

One of our clients, Waste Connections, Inc., has over 500 locations across the United States and Canada. The company has 21,000 employees and is worth nearly $5 billion. Leadership at Waste Connections designed and implemented a *sustainable high-performance culture that people want to be a part of*—and it has a remarkable record of responsible, sustainable growth as a result.

"Culture, and specifically the values that support a culture of servant leadership, are the fundamental pillars on which our company has been built. Those values are what this company lives and dies on on a daily basis. They're the thread that runs through the company and holds everything together, so that people know exactly what they can and should expect of each other, up and down the organization. Our aim is to make all of our decisions on a daily basis, be they short- or long-term decisions, in alignment with those values. That's not just a standard for leadership. That is a standard for everyone."

—Ron Mittelstaedt, CEO, Waste Connections

In the pages that follow, you will be hearing more about Waste Connections and other organizations that have built and protected a high-performance culture. For now, just understand this: if Waste Connections is not too big for this, your organization is not too big for this.

THERE REALLY IS ONE CURE FOR ALL THOSE PAINS IN THE BUTT

It is natural to feel skeptical in the early going. But it is also important to commit to exploring new ways of thinking when it comes to organizational culture. What we will be exploring together is a proven system. It works. It transforms your pains in the butt into sustainable competitive advantages in all eleven of the areas we looked at in the previous chapter. We have seen it happen multiple times, in multiple industries, in good times and bad. This is not a miracle, and it is not a trick. It is a process, it is repeatable, and it works—because it identifies and systematizes the cure for all eleven of those business challenges: *accountability.*

> The cure for all eleven of the business challenges we looked at in the previous chapter is ACCOUNTABILITY.

If we want to know what is standing between us and a high-performance culture…the kind of culture that everyone wants to be part of and wants to support…it is this: *a lack of accountability in our working culture.*

Accountability must be a *cultural* reality, an ongoing experience in your organization. It cannot be something that materializes only when leadership does not get what it wants from someone.

The success that Waste Connections and scores of other companies we've worked with have created is rooted in that one powerful, much-misunderstood word: *accountability.* Their results derive from making accountability a core element of the daily working culture. That means adopting a whole new paradigm and creating a whole new reality— an accountable reality—for yourself, your team, and everyone your organization touches.

But here is the problem: That does not happen by accident. It happens only on purpose.

In order to experience a sustainable high-performance culture that people want to be a part of, we must first design it—on purpose. We have to *build* it for a purpose. And we have to *defend* it with purpose.

> In order to experience a sustainable high-performance culture that people want to be a part of, we must first design it—on purpose. We have to *build* it for a purpose. And we have to *defend* it with purpose.

The kind of culture we are talking about does not happen on its own. It requires conscious thought. It requires commitment. And it requires leadership.

THE TWO TYPES OF CULTURE

As it turns out, there are two types of culture. There is a culture by default, and there is a culture by design. A culture by default is what many organizations have. A culture by design is what Waste Connections and the other organizations whose stories I will be sharing with you here have built and defended. And it took effort.

Lots of leaders I talk to have *tried* to have a culture by design, but they end up having a culture by default—also known as a lowest-common-denominator culture, or a culture where anything goes. The reason that they do not have a culture by design is that they do not have a process for creating, implementing, and defending that culture. They are not even aware that there is such a process.

So what happens? How does a culture by default take root? It happens because leaders take the easy way out.

Leaders do not confront the situation. They do not want to make waves. They share a couple of stories about what they think the culture should be, circulate a few emails, tack up a few posters, make some mandates, and hope that does the trick. They think their people have "got it" when they have not "got it." *The reality that leaders do not "get it" is evidenced in the leaders' lack of accountability to their own people.*

> The reality that leaders do not "get it" is evidenced in the leaders' lack of accountability to their own people.

To put it bluntly, people at organizations where there is a culture by default do not do what they say they are going to do. That dysfunctional dynamic is hardwired into the organization. It is a culture of cowardice. And the cowardice starts at the very top of the organization. The *leader* is unaccountable because the leader is afraid to do what they know they should do due to a fear of the short-term bottom-line ramifications. This fear is misguided. It is based on false assumptions. And it dooms the culture.

> "What is a fear of living? ...It is not doing what you came here to do, out of timidity and spinelessness. The antidote is to take full responsibility for yourself—for the time you take up and the space you occupy. If you don't know what you're here to do, then just do some good." —Maya Angelou

Make no mistake—this lack of courage on the part of the leader is what leads to a culture by default. Fear is the root cause of an unaccountable culture, a culture where people do not do what they say they are going to do, to the detriment of relationships.

A culture by design, on the other hand, is an accountable culture where people make relational commitments and keep them *no matter what*. They do what they say they are going to do.

> A culture by default is an unaccountable culture, a culture where people do not do what they say they are going to do, to the detriment of relationships. A culture by design is an accountable culture where people make relational commitments and keep them *no matter what*. They do what they say they are going to do.

CLOSE-UP: CULTURE BY DEFAULT

Here is an example of what an organizational culture by default looks like in practice. A consulting firm I know of tells clients, prospective clients, members of the media, and anyone else who will listen that they are all about "excellence, professionalism, and commitment to people." If you just read their press releases and did nothing else, you would think that that is what their culture is all about.

But here's the big question: Is that what people actually *experience* while they are working at this consulting firm? I am going to say no, and here is why. A while back, I was talking to one of the senior partners at that consulting firm. I'll call him Guy. Here is what Guy said to me:

"Sam, you know that growth bottleneck you and I were talking about a couple of months ago? Well, we solved the problem. We figured out how we can manage the workload. We have finally got it all figured out. What we are going to do is we are going to hire consultants full time but not put them on the partner track. And then, if there's a business downturn, we are going to just let them all go."

Does that kind of decision-making say "excellence" to you? Or does it say, "We're all about short-term fixes, and we don't care about people and the impact those fixes have on people's lives"?

Does that kind of decision-making say "professionalism" to you? Or does it say, "We cut corners whenever and wherever necessary"?

Does that kind of decision-making say "commitment to people" to you? Or does it say, "We cannot be trusted—so you had better watch your own back, because no one else is going to be watching it"?

That is what a culture by default—a low-commitment culture—looks like. Guy sees people as a means to an end. He does not care about what their needs are. He does not care about what their interests are. All he cares about is generating a profit for his firm and getting his share. That is what he is modeling for the rest of the organization. And that is what he will get back: *I look out for me, not for the team.*

Guy is like a lot of leaders who get complacent because they are doing well financially. They think they are making smart decisions that are best for the organization and its bottom line. They get sucked into believing that making money, or even leading their industry, means they are as good as they can be. But here is the problem: the leaders of organizations where there is a low-commitment culture typically get passed up by the competition…and do not realize what has happened for months or even years!

Very often, the leaders at organizations that operate under a culture by default think they are on track because they are making money or because they stack up well when compared to others in their industry. What they may not realize, though, is that:

- An accountable organizational culture—a culture by design—would deliver **better** financial results than they are currently experiencing.

- An accountable organizational culture would also deliver more **sustainable** results, meaning that the organization would perform at a high level during both good times and bad.

- An accountable organizational culture would **make the competition irrelevant.** In a true culture by design, a culture built on making and keeping commitments that support relationships, you are competing only against yourself. You are always trying to improve, to discover your real potential and grow to achieve that potential, and to deepen relationships. Clients and customers notice that, and they appreciate it. So they stick around.

How, then, do you make sure that your organization is driven by an accountable culture, an organizational culture where people consistently make and keep commitments that honor and support relationships? We will look at that question in the next chapter.

Chapter 3

Two Things You Need to Know About a Culture by Design

THERE ARE TWO VITALLY IMPORTANT THINGS you need to know about living an organizational culture by design—an accountable, sustainable, high-performance culture that people want to be a part of. The first is that it starts with you. The second is that there is a clear, comprehensible, proven process you can follow in order to make this kind of culture a reality in your organization.

Let's look at each of those points in turn.

First, *accountability starts with you.*

> ## Accountability starts with you.

That means the person you see in the mirror in the morning is the key to making this work.

Accountability means doing what you say you are going to do—making commitments and keeping them—no matter what. That is not something you can layer onto your organization or your team from the outside. It is something they need to see from the leader. Which is you.

Every leader we talk to—every single one—wants accountability to produce better results for them and for their organization. BUT…they often do not get the improvement they are looking for. The question is HOW to make the results we want a reality.

Here is how *not* to do it: tell people you are going to start holding them accountable for X, Y, or Z.

The whole idea of "holding someone accountable" is misguided. It simply does not work. When people hear you talking about holding them accountable, they go into self-protective mode. They think they are about to be attacked. And you know what? They are right. Telling people you are holding them accountable *always* backfires. You know what does not backfire? *You* making a commitment to *them*…and then keeping it.

> ### Accountability cannot be mandated.
> ### It can only be inspired.

Accountability cannot be mandated. It can only be inspired. And the leader is the perfect person to inspire it. How? By making and keeping commitments to the team as a whole and to the individuals on the team.

There are two kinds of commitments leaders make that are relevant to our discussion here: tactical and relational. Tactical commitments are day-to-day items on the to-do list. They come and they go. For instance, making sure people get paid is a tactical commitment. Does it need to happen? Yes. Is it your responsibility? Yes. Does it create accountability? No. Because it is an item on the to-do list. There is no meaningful emotional connection between people when it happens. There is only a negative emotional deficit between people when it does not happen!

Bottom line: Tactical commitments are important; we want to be sure to honor them. Organizations and teams cannot function without them. But just fulfilling tactical commitments is *not* the way to inspire your team or your organization to be accountable, to be and do their very best. And it is not how you build an accountable culture. We are responsible for things, but we are accountable to people. When we make and keep a commitment that supports a relationship, THAT IS ACCOUNTABILITY.

Relational commitments, therefore, are the path you want to take if you are serious about inspiring accountability in your team and your organization. These are the commitments—sometimes spoken, sometimes not—that support your *relationship* with another person, whether or not you talk about those commitments.

There are ten core relational commitments that transcend the to-do list and, when honored consistently, create a powerful emotional bond between you and the person to whom you make the commitment. That emotional bond inspires accountability.

The ten core relational commitments that create accountability in you and inspire accountability in others are listed below.

THE TEN NON-NEGOTIABLE RELATIONAL COMMITMENTS THAT CREATE ACCOUNTABILITY

A *relational commitment* is a commitment that serves a relationship with one or more people. The ten core relational commitments appear below. All are non-negotiable for accountable leaders.

I COMMIT TO HELPING INDIVIDUALS REACH THEIR POTENTIAL AND BE THEIR BEST. When my people know I care about their growth and development, they care about the organization's growth and development.

I COMMIT TO TRUTH. Lying and accountability cannot coexist.

I COMMIT TO LIVING THE VALUES. Our organization's non-negotiable core values state our shared principles and our standards of behavior.

I COMMIT TO "IT'S ALL OF US." I accept that if the other person fails, I fail, and I do not succeed unless the other person succeeds.

I COMMIT TO EMBRACING FAULTS AND FAILURES AS WELL AS OPPORTUNITIES AND SUCCESSES. I am not perfect, and I do not expect others to be perfect.

I COMMIT TO SOUND FINANCIAL PRINCIPLES. This commitment is all about stewardship and making wise decisions with our financial resources.

I COMMIT TO A SAFE SPACE. This commitment is about creating and sustaining an environment of physical, emotional, and psychological safety.

I COMMIT TO "MY WORD IS MY BOND." What we say must align with what we do. If I say it, people can depend on it.

I COMMIT TO STANDING WITH YOU WHEN ALL HELL BREAKS LOOSE. No matter what happens in the lives of the people I lead, I am there for them when they most need support.

I COMMIT TO A GOOD REPUTATION. Our actions matter—not just in the outcomes we deliver today, but in what people say about us, our organization, and our team tomorrow. I always make decisions that protect our good name.

Here is the bottom line: if you are not willing to make all ten of these relational commitments to your people, and keep those commitments no matter what, then you cannot expect your team to be accountable to you, to each other, to your customers, or to the organization. It is that simple.

> If you are not willing to make all ten of these relational commitments to your people, and keep those commitments no matter what, then you cannot expect your team to be accountable to you, to each other, to your customers, or to the organization.

The big question is—how do you build and defend a culture around those commitments? This question brings us to the second thing you need to know about a culture by design.

THE FIVE-STEP ACCOUNTABILITY ADVANTAGE™ PROCESS FOR CREATING A COMPETITIVE CULTURAL ADVANTAGE

The big point to bear in mind when it comes to building and defending an accountable culture is *you cannot wing it.* To make this work, your culture must be an extension of what you really believe. And our experience has shown that many leaders need, but do not have, a process to make that happen.

Simply announcing the new culture by means of a flashy email, or poster, or video, or some combination of the three will not work. No matter how snappy your headline, no matter how good your intentions, no matter how compelling the graphic design you attach to this initiative, *it will not stick*—meaning it will not affect people's perceptions, perspectives, and behaviors—unless you follow the five steps listed below with care and courage. They are the five distinct steps to building a high-performance culture.

> There are five distinct steps to building a high-performance culture.

STEP ONE: DEFINE THE CULTURE.

- What are the values that drive your actions and decisions? (Not someone else's—yours.) How do you know?
- What are the values that drive your working culture? (Not another organization's—yours.) How do you know?

STEP TWO: MODEL THE CULTURE.

- Do leaders embody, align with, and live by the stated non-negotiable values?
- How do you know?

STEP THREE: TEACH THE CULTURE.

- Do leaders, and others, teach the values on a daily basis?
- How do you know?

STEP FOUR: PROTECT THE CULTURE.

- What happens when someone in your organization makes a decision or takes a course of action that does not support the stated non-negotiable values?
- What happens when someone in your organization PERSISTENTLY makes decisions and/or takes courses of action that do not support the stated non-negotiable values?
- How do you know that happens?

STEP FIVE: CELEBRATE THE CULTURE.

- Who is celebrated, and why, in this organization?
- Does leadership value people?
- How do you know?

If you have tried in the past to improve your organizational culture but have made little or no headway, *it is time to try something different.* Do not walk away from that attempt. Refine it. Take what you have done already and look at it closely. Learn from it. Then *use* what you have learned firsthand about what did and did not work as you implement this five-step process. It is proven. It is tested. It works.

> "Every defeat, every loss, every heartbreak contains its own seed, its own lesson on how to improve your performance next time." —Malcolm X

Now that you have a brief overview of the five steps, you are ready for a deeper dive. In the next section of the book, we will look closely at Defining the Culture. This is the essential first step, the step without which nothing else happens, to get you closer to a high-performance culture that people want to be a part of.

II

Define the
CULTURE

Chapter 4

What Are the Values?

DEFINING THE CULTURE starts with defining the values. And make no mistake: if you are the senior leader, they start with *your* values.

By the way, if you are *not* the senior leader, what you value still matters deeply to your organization and to everyone your organization touches. But if you are the senior leader, what you value is the *primary influence* on the organization's working culture. That means you want to spend some time on this.

Most organizations—most people—have *not* taken the time to define their values. Many people we work with *tell us* that they have done this, when actually they have been doing something else—public relations! Saying trendy words (like *Integrity* and *Respect*) that are meant to sound appealing to the outside world, but that do not actually guide your behavior and decisions, is not the same thing as defining *your* values.

> To define your value set, you must work the process.

To define your value set, you must work the process. This is the first step of the Accountability Advantage™ process. If you are the senior leader, it is vitally important that you and your team execute this first part of the process properly…because if you do not, nothing you do later on in steps two through five will have much impact on your organization. The culture by default will continue to prevail, and the behaviors and outcomes will not change in any meaningful, sustainable way. *Work the process* laid out in this section of the book, even when it takes you beyond what is comfortable or familiar.

> "A good process produces good results." —Nick Saban

Let's look closely now at the five key facts you need to know if you are serious about supporting and implementing this process…and defining your values.

FIVE KEY FACTS ABOUT VALUES

FACT #1: A non-negotiable core value is something that is so important to you that if you lost it, you would move heaven and earth to find it. Your principles or standards of behavior—what is truly important in life—are encapsulated in your values. Organizational values are the answer to the question, "How do we do things and make decisions around here?" Personal values are the answer to the question, "How do I do things and how do I make decisions in my life?" In this book, whenever we talk about a value, we mean a non-negotiable core value—a standard of behavior that respects the rights of others and is absolute. If you are not willing to adopt that definition, if you are not willing to stand behind what you believe to that degree, please do not call it a value!

> A non-negotiable core value is a standard of behavior that respects the rights of others and is absolute. It is something that is so important to you that if you lost it, you would move heaven and earth to find it.

FACT #2: Both sets of values are in play here if you are the senior leader. If you are the founder, CEO, owner, president, head honcho—fill in the blank with the title of your choice—both of these value sets matter immensely. Both sets must be clarified and codified (which is a big part of what you will be doing in this chapter). Both need to be modeled consistently for the important people in your life. If you are a solo entrepreneur, you can and should take the initiative to identify both sets of values, ensuring as you do so that they align with each other. If you are the senior leader of an organization with one or more teams who look to you for leadership, you must first identify *your personal values* (using the process you'll find in this chapter), and then you must lead the conversation about what the organizational values are with a cross-section of people in your organization.

FACT #3: Your actions and choices—not your words—determine whether you have a given value. Translation: You must live your values. It is critical to talk about your values, but it is even more important to live them. If you say that one of your values is *Honesty*, for instance, but you then knowingly lie to someone, you have lost that value. You can work to regain it, but if you choose to ignore it, you do not have that value.

FACT #4: For your values to be complete they need to connect to your actions in four specific areas.

- **Foundational values** are the basis or groundwork on which everything else stands. (For instance, **Integrity.**) Foundational values speak to your character.

- **Relational values** define the way in which two or more people behave toward each other. (Notice that **Integrity** can be expressed as both a foundational value and a relational value.) In any organization, there needs to be both internal and external relational values. Lots of companies are great when it comes to defining the external relational values, meaning the ones that customers experience. But if they overlook the internal relational values and never define those, there is going to be a problem. You cannot deliver a better experience to a client or customer than you receive as an employee. The quality of the relationships you have with clients and customers will never exceed the quality of the relationships you have within the organization.

- **Professional values** define the level of quality and excellence with which you approach any undertaking, regardless of whether you are being paid to do it. **(Integrity, Self-Improvement,** and **Significance**—that is, the desire to create meaning and inspire others to be, do, and achieve their full potential—can all be expressed as professional values.)

- **Community values** affect how you feel about, participate in, and support your community. (**Contribution** can be expressed as a community value, and it can also be expressed as a relational value governing your interactions with others. **Integrity**, too, could be something you adopt and express as a community value.[1])

---

1   Note that the way you choose to define your values will determine which of these categories a given value falls into. Note, too, that a value may fall into two, three, or all four areas, depending on the definition and narrative you develop. In the examples I have shared with you, *Integrity* shows up in each of the four groups, but you might choose to put it only in one.

A great list of core values checks all four of these boxes, and it also features a *narrative* for each value that explains, concisely and clearly, exactly what each value means to those who work for the organization. (A single word or phrase can mean very different things to different people.) Employees do not have to be able to recite the narratives from memory. They must, however, be able to understand the values and explain them in their own words.

Anything less than what I have just established may be a great *start*...but it is not a great *set* of values.

FACT #5: The values we identify, live, and protect matter deeply to the organization. A culture by default emerges when we fail to identify, live, and protect the values that support the specific working culture we are aiming to create. A culture by design emerges when we define, model, and protect our values.

The process of identifying our values is not automatic. It requires both careful self-assessment and careful organizational assessment. If we simply "adopt" someone else's values, or some other organization's values, they will not stick (for us or anyone else) and they will not have any impact on decisions, behaviors, or outcomes. This is because *our actions will always follow our beliefs, not someone else's beliefs.*

> **Our actions will always follow our beliefs.**

Now that you have a sense of what the values landscape looks like, you are ready to take action and start defining yours. This should be considered a mandatory step if you are the senior leader in the organization and a recommended step for everyone else.

On a separate sheet of paper or in a word processing document, you will want to take some time to write down answers to each of the following questions:

Question One: Who Are Your Heroes?

Write down the names of five of your heroes. These should be people who have inspired you and made you think, "Hey, I really want to be like that person." You may have known them personally; you may not have. The people on your list could be living or dead. They could be fictional or real. All that matters is that the person is someone you admire deeply, someone whose example has made a difference for you and who has emerged as a role model.

So, for example, you might include the following people on your list:

- Abraham Lincoln
- My grandfather
- Spider-Man's Uncle Ben
- Marie Curie
- Martin Luther King

Question Two: Why Are Those People Your Heroes?

Next to each of those names you just listed, I want you to write at least five words or brief phrases that describe specific PERSONAL QUALITIES or TRAITS that made you choose that person for your list. So, for instance, if Lincoln is one of your heroes and you are inspired by his quote "I am not bound to win, but I am bound to be true; I am not bound to succeed, but I am bound to live up to what light I have," then you might lead your list with the word *Integrity*. Your full list for Lincoln might look like this:

Abraham Lincoln:

- Integrity
- Committed to His Cause
- Eloquent
- Kept Things Together No Matter What
- Strong in Adversity
- Wise
- Saw the Big Picture

Do this for all five names on your list. Again, notice that even though you never knew Lincoln personally, or never could know Spider-Man's Uncle Ben in real life, you can identify the ways of acting, thinking, communicating, and making decisions they displayed that have had a positive impact on you—the traits of theirs that have made you think, "I want to be like that."

The words you list for each figure should answer the question: *Why them?*

When you get done with question two, you should have at least twenty-five qualities listed—at least five for each person you have chosen.

Question Three: Where Are You Right Now in Relation to Their Qualities?

For each of the qualities you listed, I want you to rate—honestly— where you are right now in your life with regard to living that quality on a scale of one to ten. Be tough on yourself here. The only person who will read this sheet is you. Give yourself an accurate assessment in each area. Understand that a score of 10/10 means you never deviate from the highest standard set by your hero in that area.

Ask yourself, in every area where you do not give yourself a 10 out of 10, why you gave yourself the score you did and what you would need to do to reach a score of 10 out of 10.

Once you have done that, I want you to underline the one quality for each hero that you most wish you had in your life.

Your list for Lincoln might now look like this:

Abraham Lincoln:

- **Integrity (7/10)**
- Committed to His Cause (6/10)
- Eloquent (7/10)
- Kept Things Together No Matter What (8/10)
- Strong in Adversity (6/10)
- Wise (6/10)
- Saw the Big Picture (6/10)

Question Four: What Are the Five Qualities You Have Underlined?

Review your long list and use it to create a shorter list of five underlined traits or qualities, one from each person you've chosen as a hero.

Your list should now look something like this:

- Abraham Lincoln: Integrity
- My grandfather: Respect
- Spider-Man's Uncle Ben: Contribution
- Marie Curie: Self-Improvement
- Martin Luther King: Significance

Congratulations. You have just created a first-draft list of your core values. That is a start. But it is not the end!

Question Five: What Does the Second Draft of Your List Look Like?

Using the first-draft list you have already developed, your next job is to check how well it matches up with the following four value categories and revise it so that it fulfills all four. You may need to go back and use words you have developed earlier in the process to do this.

Which of the words on your list is your foundational value? Foundational values are the basis or groundwork on which everything else stands. They identify the one thing you will never, ever compromise on. (For Lincoln, that value was *Integrity*.) Foundational values speak to your character.

To identify your foundational values, consider writing down your best answers to these questions:

- *What defines your character?*
- *What is the one thing you will never compromise on?*
- *What standard would you say is critically important to you in living the life you are supposed to lead?*

Which of the words on your list are relational values? These values affect the way in which two or more people behave toward each other. Notice that *Integrity* can be expressed as both a foundational value and a relational value.

To identify your relational values, consider writing down your best answers to these questions:

- *What do you believe about people?*

- *What do you value most in your relationships with family and friends? Why?*

- *What values do you think your family and friends see in you? Why?*

- *What do you value most in your relationships with your colleagues? Why?*

- *What values do you think your colleagues see in you?*

Which of the words on your list are professional values? Note that you can and do have professional values, whether or not you have a job. Your professional values determine the level of quality and excellence you deliver, regardless of what you happen to be doing or whether you are being paid to do it. Note that *Integrity*, *Self-Improvement*, and *Significance* can all be expressed as professional values.

To identify your professional values, consider writing down your best answers to these questions:

- *What do you believe about excellence?*

- *What values help you be better at fulfilling your responsibilities in your career/professional life?*

- *Why are those values important to you?*

- *What values point you toward excellence in everything you do?*

- *Why are those values important to you?*

Which of the words on your list are community values? These values affect how you feel about, participate in, and support your community. Note that *Contribution* can be expressed as a community value, and it can also be expressed as a relational value governing your interactions with others.

To identify your community values, consider writing down your best answers to these questions:

- *What do you believe about community?*
- *How do you define your community?*
- *What do you value in the community? Why?*
- *What brings you joy when it comes to taking action that makes your community better?*

This next part is important: A great list of core values checks all four of these boxes! Revise your list until it does.

This may mean tweaking the number of core values on your list. After you spend some time following the steps I have laid out here, you may end up deciding that you need only three values and that those three values address the foundational, relational, professional, and community questions I have just raised. You may end up deciding that you need many more than three values. I have seen powerful lists that used twenty values. Do what works best for you and your organization.

Once your list checks all four boxes, you will have a viable second draft of your list of core values.

But that is not the end of the process!

Question Six: What Is the Narrative for Each of Your Core Values?

Just writing down a list of words is not enough to establish your core values—not by a long shot. For one thing, each word you have chosen needs to be clearly defined so that it is obvious what unique meaning it carries for you. What you mean by *Integrity* may be very different from what someone else means. Not only that, but the meanings of your core values are likely to become clearer to you over time. You need a values narrative. A narrative, in this context, is a written statement of what you DO to make sure the values show up in your world. The narrative helps you to get the key distinctions down on paper now so that you can review them a month from now, a year from now, or a decade from now and make whatever changes are necessary in light of your overall life experience and any new perspectives you've gained over time. In writing the narrative and gaining clarity about what each value means to you, you will also gain deeper insight on which values fall into which of the four categories I have shared with you: foundational, relational, professional, and community. Remember, one value can attach to one, several, or all four of the categories.

Here is the narrative that supports my values. Use it to get a clear sense of what a values narrative looks like. Do not use it as something you can cut and paste into a file and adopt as your own without thinking about it. Do use it as a model for bringing your own core values to life.

Integrity

> I make decisions based on the belief that my word is my bond and doing what is right is always the right thing to do. I commit to this no matter what.

Respect

> I see all people as equal. I value other people's opinions, appreciate their beliefs, and recognize the importance of their priorities.

Significance

> I create meaning in my life and the lives of the people around me. I look for ways to create significance for my family. I make the effort to get to know people. I look for potential in the people with whom I come in contact. I encourage people. I participate in my community and work to make a difference.
>
> Life is an adventure. I actively live that adventure when I live with integrity, respect, and significance.

Remember: Only when your actions align with your core values are the values yours. If you look back at the end of a day and find you made no decisions that align with your core values, there is something you need to fix. Values are not something that you want to achieve at some point in the future. They are right now. Values and beliefs are interconnected. Values are beliefs in action. Beliefs are inward facing. Values are outward facing. Your values and beliefs are always reflected in your actions.

Values and beliefs are interconnected.

Values and beliefs determine your decisions *right now*.

Values are beliefs in action.

Beliefs are inward facing.

Values are outward facing.

Your values and beliefs are
always reflected in your actions.

THE PERSONAL VALUES EXERCISE
IS NON-NEGOTIABLE

It is no exaggeration to say that what I just shared with you is the foundation of organizational accountability.

Everyone should take the time and make the investment in themselves to discover and define in writing what their values are. If you are the leader of the organization, you must have clarity about your own values before you can lead the conversation about values at an organizational level. If you hold a different title or no title at all, you also will need to work through this exercise, because once you have the clarity that written values bring, you will be in a better position to align what you believe with the organization's values.

Getting Ready for a Bigger Conversation about Values

If you are the senior leader, you will have a strong sense of your own personal values once you complete the steps I just outlined. You will understand the standards and practices by which you operate, not just in terms of your professional goals, but in all aspects of your life. You will know the answer to this question:

What are the values that drive your actions and decisions? (Not someone else's—yours.)

Not only that, but you will be able explain what each of those values means to you, using your values narrative.

Once you know your own values, your job is to *share* all you have done with your team members—those you work with personally, on a regular basis, and who look to you for leadership—and get them to do the same exercise you just did. Make it mandatory. *There is no way to design an organization's culture without the senior leader and their team knowing what they value.* So support them as they make the same journey you just made; help them get the same level of clarity you now have. Just as important—*learn what they value and why!*

> There is no way to design an organization's culture without the senior leader and their team knowing what they value.

This may take just a day or two if you plan on spending some time together to work intensively on this, or it may take longer than that if you want to expand the timeframe a little bit. Either way works. At the end of the process, you will have developed a clear sense of what *each* team member's personal values are, because *each* of your team members will have their own personal values narrative. This is important for three reasons:

- The team members will now have seen the leader taking the first step of defining and sharing their personal values, which means the leader is modeling an important best practice. Here as elsewhere in an accountable culture, **the leader goes first, inspiring their people to grow, learn, and become their very best self.**

- The team members will be in a position to speak up if and when they find themselves in a situation where there is a possibility that the leader may be about to compromise a stated personal value. (It happens more commonly than you might think.) For instance, if the leader says he values innovation, but he will not consider a new way of accomplishing an important goal, the team member can reference his value and offer a gentle reminder. Of course, this works in the opposite direction as well: the senior leader can always remind a team member of a stated value he or she may have overlooked.

- Last but not least, everyone in the leader's inner circle now has a sense of what their individual values are. They have experienced this powerful discovery themselves—and can now help lead the larger conversation about the **organizational** values. However, it is not **just** the executive team that will be taking part in that conversation.

What is next? You will find out in chapter 5.

Get Everyone in the Room!

AS WE HAVE SEEN, the leader and the entire executive team must first "walk the walk" in terms of clarifying their own personal values. Once they do that, their job is to broaden the conversation. They will want to invest time, attention, and energy in real-time discussions with others in the organization in order to find the answer to the following vitally important questions:

- *What are the values that drive our working culture? (Not another organization's—ours.)*

- *How do we know?*

The same process you used to identify the *individual* values will now guide you as you identify the *organizational* values. Because this conversation affects the entire organization, it must involve a lot more people. How many people? Here is the two-part answer, which surprises a lot of senior leaders:

- If your organization employs more than 50 people, then we recommend that the senior leader select a cross-section of team members, chosen to represent the entire organization.

You want these employees to participate side by side with the executive team in these discussions. Make sure every department is represented; make sure no team has any evidence to support the belief that their voice was not heard or their ears were not privy to the conversation. The idea here is to get the functional equivalent of having **everyone in the room.** Each individual taking part will be encouraged to share the details of the discussion with anyone and everyone they work with. This is not a secret meeting!

- If your organization employs 50 people or fewer, the answer is much simpler: Just get everyone in the room for this discussion. Period.

We have led this process more times than we can count, and one of the things we have learned is that many senior leaders, with the best of intentions, will push back when they are asked to extend this conversation as outlined above. They hesitate when they hear they need to get everyone, or a cross-section representing everyone, in the room at the same time.

Sometimes they will share logistical or practical concerns like:

- *"This is really important, and I don't want to have to manage that many moving parts."*
- *"This may take a lot of time, and I don't want people off the job for that long."*

Sometimes they will express concerns that indicate a desire to formalize a set of values they already feel strongly about by saying things like:

- *"I already know what I want, and I already know who gets what I am talking about. That's why I want to limit this*

> *discussion to the people I know for sure have the 'right values' and the 'right approach' to working for this organization."*

- *"We have already done the heavy lifting. That's why I want the executive team to create the list of values and the rest of the organization to just offer feedback on it. That will keep the list from being watered down and losing meaning and impact."*

Sometimes they will try to sidestep perceived personnel or political problems by saying things like:

- *"There are a couple of bad apples in departments X and Y, and we don't want them taking this discussion off track."*

News flash: All of these responses amount to cherry-picking. And all of them will sabotage your efforts to design, create, and protect an accountable working culture.

Why? Because cherry-picking is the opposite of diversity, equity, and inclusion, which is what you need to make this work.

> Cherry-picking is the opposite of diversity, equity, and inclusion, which is what you need to make this work.

Promise: You will have fewer logistical problems and massively higher productivity down the road…but only if you include the entire organization in this conversation.

Promise: You will not end up with "bad values" or a "poor work standard" by including everyone. That simply does not happen. People who are included in this conversation want to work to a higher standard, and they want to work with other people who want to work to a higher standard.

Promise: You will get new insights and ideas that clarify your own thinking about the values…but only if you include the entire organization in this conversation.

Promise: You will be better equipped to deal with the (so-called) bad apples…but only if you include the entire organization in this conversation. (We will have much more to say about the "bad apple" problem in later chapters.)

> "We must learn to live together as brothers and sisters or perish together as fools."
> —Dr. Martin Luther King, Jr.

Bottom line: YOU DO NOT WANT JUST YOUR BUDDIES IN THE ROOM FOR THIS CONVERSATION. That is the surest and quickest way to kill the cultural initiative into which you are investing your time, your effort, your attention, and yes, your financial resources to launch. If even *one* team does not feel represented…or does not feel listened to…or has any reason to conclude that all of this talk about values is just something the higher-ups have come up with in order to get what they want from the rest of us, *you will slip back into a culture by default.* And that is not what you want.

We were working with a CEO not long ago who led a company that had only three executives and a total of twenty-six employees. This CEO had assumed that the discussion that defined his organization's values was going to be something that involved just him and the other two executives. We pushed back and said, "Let's include all of your people in the discussion. In fact, we won't take on this project if you don't include them."

He said, "I never even thought of that."

We explained: "If we bring everyone in, then everyone has a chance to be heard. They need to be more than just symbolically there; they need to be participants in the conversation. Everyone has to have a chance to be heard. We need to aggressively pursue everyone's thoughts and insights on what the values should look like for this company. If we do that, everyone will own it—and everyone will live the values."

He brought everyone into the room. And he ended up being glad he did!

Here is the point: if you do it the other way, if you limit the discussion to what the senior executives and their buddies think the organizational values are, *this process will not work.*

You will get 100 percent buy-in from the people on the executive team and zero buy-in from everyone else in the organization. It may not look like that is what is happening when you post the list of values on the bulletin board. People may smile and nod their heads. But that will be meaningless. Your people will not own the process or the results. They will assume this is the new "flavor of the week." And they will be right. The culture and the outcomes will not change.

Remember: Diversity always starts with diversity of thought. You want to put diversity of thought—as well as every other kind of diversity—to work for your organization. You want everyone to have a voice. The more different backgrounds, perspectives, and life stories you have as this meeting begins, the better the discussion is going to be.

So get everyone in the room, and task them with helping you to create the value set and the organizational values narrative!

(Sidenote: What ultimately shows up in your organizational values narrative may overlap verbatim with your personal values list, but it does not have to.)

WARNING: THIS IS NOT JUST ONE VALUE

Notice that we are talking about a value *set,* not just a single value. This is vitally important.

You want multiple points of clarity about what is important to your organization, not just one point of clarity. People need to be able to make sure that what they are doing—the actions they are taking, the decisions they are making—lines up with *everything* on the list. If you define just one value or if you define a number of values but only ever emphasize one that you feel is particularly important, your organization is going to run into problems.

Let's take a moment and look at how those problems might arise.

Say you and everyone else in the room come up with these five values:

> We make decisions from a place of integrity.
>
> We believe in aggressive growth and act to make it a reality.
>
> We respect each other and our customers.
>
> We give back to the community in which we live.
>
> We are a learning-driven organization committed to excellence and to continuous personal and professional improvement.

Now, assuming that everyone in the room has signed off on these five elements, this value set is a good start. I say "a good start" because each of these sentences still needs more elaboration in the form of a values narrative that makes it abundantly clear, both to current team members and to newcomers who may come along, exactly what we mean by words like "integrity" and "respect." But these will do for now. The point is, you have identified five important points on the values map.

But what if you ignored four of those values?

Suppose all the senior leader ever talked about, acknowledged, and rewarded was that second value, *We believe in aggressive growth and act to make it a reality*?

Suppose that three months from the time everyone agreed on the five values, it was only the one that focused on aggressive growth that anyone ever took action on?

Suppose that even though the other four values appeared in memos and emails and on the bulletin board in the coffee lounge, people simply forgot that they existed?

Suppose people stopped noticing when they acted out of alignment with those four values?

Sooner or later, you'd have a potential crisis to deal with. Whenever people in your organization pursued aggressive growth without asking themselves, *Am I making decisions from a place of integrity?*—the organization would begin to go off track. Whenever they pursued aggressive growth without asking how *Respect* fit into their decision-making, or giving back, or learning, the organization would go even further off track. And eventually you would be looking at a situation where the one "value" led to a dysfunctional working environment.

The point is, that second value is fine, and it is great to have it on the list if you and your team believe it belongs there. Just make sure you isolate and define *all* the values that point to the best of your organization's past experience and future potential. Then commit to live the *whole* value set! There is never a "lead" value or a "main" value. All values have equal weight. We must live them all fully and equally.

> There is never a "lead" value or a "main" value. All values have equal weight. We must live them all fully and equally.

THE GROUP CONVERSATION ABOUT VALUES: FOUR KEY DELIVERABLES

I cannot overemphasize how important this group conversation is. As a result of this discussion, four extraordinary and powerful things must happen:

- The group must isolate and develop the narrative for **multiple values** that define, in a concise and compelling way, "how we do things around here."

- Each individual member of the group must sign on with the reality that the values, as defined, are basic requirements for working at this organization. In other words, if you cannot live the values, then you cannot work here. If the group is a cross-section of the team members in the organization, specific team members must be tasked with the duty of sharing this fact with others on their team so that **everyone in the organization** is clear that these are now the values everyone—top to bottom, side to side, full-time or otherwise—is now accepting as "how we do things around here." If that makes the process take a little longer so the rest of the organization can catch up, so be it. The conversation continues in conjunction with the leader's personal commitment to these values…until *everyone* buys into the values.

- The entire organization, meaning every team member on every team, must not only buy into the values with words, but they also must be willing, able, *and supported* to protect the values with both words and actions. We will talk more about protecting the values in later chapters, but for now, just understand that during this session, people *at all levels* must be empowered to speak up when they see someone acting out of alignment with the values. Which they will!

- Last but certainly not least, each and every person taking part in this conversation must be able to describe authentically why each value is important and worth protecting, how the value applies to the work they do on a daily basis, how the values support each other, and why all the values are equally non-negotiable.

Do not number the values. No value is more important than any other. They are all in play all the time…so commit to living them all!

Do not number the values. No value is more important than any other. They are all in play all the time…so commit to living them all!

YOU NOW HAVE THE BASICS

If you have done everything outlined thus far, you have a clear set of organizational values in place—values that people feel they own and can buy into.

It is at this point that *leadership* will want to do a personal reality check. If we are leaders, we must make absolutely sure we are living the relational commitments. Remember: each member of the team needs to know that leadership is personally committed to them *before* they can commit to the values. You will remember these commitments from chapter 3, but here they are again for easy reference. No matter what industry you are in or what group you serve, no matter how large or small your organization is, you will want to make sure you are living all ten of these commitments on a daily basis.

THE TEN NON-NEGOTIABLE RELATIONAL COMMITMENTS THAT CREATE ACCOUNTABILITY

A *relational commitment* is a commitment that serves a relationship with one or more people. The ten core relational commitments appear below. All are non-negotiable for accountable leaders.

I COMMIT TO HELPING INDIVIDUALS REACH THEIR POTENTIAL AND BE THEIR BEST. When my people know I care about their growth and development, they care about the organization's growth and development.

I COMMIT TO TRUTH. Lying and accountability cannot coexist.

I COMMIT TO LIVING THE VALUES. Our organization's non-negotiable core values state our shared principles and our standards of behavior.

I COMMIT TO "IT'S ALL OF US." I accept that if the other person fails, I fail, and I do not succeed unless the other person succeeds.

I COMMIT TO EMBRACING FAULTS AND FAILURES AS WELL AS OPPORTUNITIES AND SUCCESSES. I am not perfect, and I do not expect others to be perfect.

I COMMIT TO SOUND FINANCIAL PRINCIPLES. This commitment is all about stewardship and making wise decisions with our financial resources.

I COMMIT TO A SAFE SPACE. This commitment is about creating and sustaining an environment of physical, emotional, and psychological safety.

I COMMIT TO "MY WORD IS MY BOND." What we say must align with what we do. If I say it, people can depend on it.

I COMMIT TO STANDING WITH YOU WHEN ALL HELL BREAKS LOOSE. No matter what happens in the lives of the people I lead, I am there for them when they most need support.

I COMMIT TO A GOOD REPUTATION. Our actions matter—not just in the outcomes we deliver today, but in what people say about us, our organization, and our team tomorrow. I always make decisions that protect our good name.

Don't number the commitments. No commitment is more important than any other. They are all in play all the time!

Don't number the commitments. No commitment is more important than any other. They are all in play all the time!

Again: These are commitments *leadership* makes to employees *first*. If we are willing to make these relational commitments to our people and then keep these commitments by taking action on them consistently, no matter what, we will have an accountable working culture. If our deeds do not match our words and our people do not feel our commitment to them, then our people will not commit to the values, or to us, or to each other, and we will *not* have an accountable working culture.

Once we *do* make and fulfill these commitments as leaders…once we *do* make a habit of living the values day after day after day…then we will have laid the foundation. We will have defined all the key elements of our working culture.

A MASTER CLASS IN ACCOUNTABILITY

As I was working on this book, it became obvious to me that I had to include one of my all-time favorite lists of organizational values in this chapter. The list in question is adapted from Happy State Bank, the remarkable organization inspired by visionary leader J. Pat Hickman. In fact, Hickman inspired *me* to refine my work to formalize a process by which organizations could come up with a glove-fitting, inspiring list of values. (Happy State Bank is the subject of my book *Non-Negotiable.)*

This book really would be incomplete without Happy State's values. You will notice, as you read them, that the list begins with a concise, powerful mission statement, a brief sequence of words with immense long-term impact that is worth leadership taking the time to develop properly.[2] You will also notice that the list reflects Pat's spiritual beliefs, which I personally consider a plus, knowing as I do that he and Happy State do not attempt to force those beliefs on anyone who does not share them.

You will also notice that the values narrative is quite long, perhaps longer than you might think you want yours to be. But when you consider that this list has enabled Happy State Bank to grow from one location in 1990 to sixty-one locations and counting today, and from $10 million in assets to almost $7 billion, I think you will begin to see that it is not the length of the list that matters. What matters is how well the list captures the values the leader is willing to live by...and inspire others to live by. I can attest from a long experience with him that Pat Hickman does indeed live these values, and he inspires others to do the same through the power of his personal example!

This list is a master class in designing an accountable, high-performance culture. Notice how the values connect to the four categories I shared with you in chapter 4: foundational, relational, professional, and community. They are covered from every angle in this

---

2   The identification of a unique organizational *purpose* that inspires people and is rooted in service, and of a *mission* that is that purpose in action, are vitally important steps. These steps are best completed, in my experience, *after* you know what your organizational values are and *after* leadership buys into and has begun to live the ten relational commitments. They are one-of-a-kind discoveries, not something that can be outlined easily in a book like this. We can help you and your organization to identify your unique purpose and the mission that supports it. Visit SamSilverstein.com for more information.

values narrative—and in a way that is impossible to misunderstand. Read it. Study it. Use it as an inspiration.

The keyword here is *inspiration*. Note that this (long) list of values reflects a great deal of work that Happy State Bank's leaders and team members did to determine what *they* believe. The list works for them. It is here to *inspire* you to create your own list by doing your own work, not to suggest that you should or could reach all the same conclusions. Your organization must find and live its own values. Cutting and pasting someone else's values is a recipe for failure.

CORE VALUES OF HAPPY STATE BANK & TRUST CO.

HAPPY STATE BANK MISSION STATEMENT

> Work hard, have fun, make money while providing outstanding customer service and following the Golden Rule.

PRINCIPLES and CORE VALUES OF HAPPY STATE BANK

Customer service is THE GOAL – go the extra mile, bend over backwards, give 100% – always greet customers with a smile – always call people by their name (the sweetest sounding word in anyone's ear is the sound of their own name) – treat every customer as if they had $1 million in the bank (we may differentiate on the rates we pay or charge but should never differentiate our service) – empower our co-owners to take care of our customers – don't let the customer leave without a smile on their face – do what is best for the customer, and sometimes that is not what is most profitable for the bank – we want to develop relationships with our customers and sincerely care about the individual customer – Great customer service is our ONLY advantage over our competition – we like co-owners who are consumed with service – how about PASSION – maintain a servant's heart – create a HAPPY EXPERIENCE

Attitude is everything – life is 10% what happens to you and 90% your attitude toward it. Give your heart, not just your words and/or your actions. Co-owners and customers can see through poor and lousy attitudes or insincerity – a good attitude is OK, but a great attitude is expected – don't let good take the place of great – be the best person that you can be

Family first – all the time, every time – THE reason one works is to provide a better life for one's family – your work will still be here tomorrow; your family grows up – while laying on a deathbed no one has ever said, "I wish I worked more" – your family really is lots more important than this bank

Treat every co-owner as well as you treat your best customer – we are on the same team; we are working for the same goals – you must assume that everyone is giving their best – and we want to bring out the best in every co-owner – go the extra mile – it's just nice to work with nice people – create a HAPPY EXPERIENCE for your co-owner

Prayer is OK – it's even encouraged – plain, flat, simple – prayer works – and while we would never force our personal spiritual beliefs on anyone, our personal spiritual beliefs guide our every decision – we would never want anyone to be uncomfortable – if you want to pray, if you are with a co-worker or customer who wants to pray, then pray

Take care of your good employees and get rid of your bad ones – pay a fair and honest wage – provide a rewarding, self-fulfilling and fun career for those who work hard and opportunities for advancement – and give others who don't share our work ethic an opportunity to flourish elsewhere – if you want "just a job," you will earn "just a paycheck" – we are looking for folks who have pride and passion and want a career – encourage the good ones and give the bad ones ideas and instructions on how to improve – there is nothing more disheartening to a good employee than to have to work next to a lousy employee – "one bad apple really can spoil the barrel" – trust the bank to be just

Respect & appreciation of others – there's no difference between officers and employees – we are all people – it's like any great championship team: at the end of the season, everyone gets a ring, even the trainers – there are skilled positions, and they may be paid more or receive more press, but it takes the whole team – and if any one person ever thinks the team can't make it without him/her, (that person is nuts) and the whole team suffers – we also want to make sure that no staff member ever feels uncomfortable, in any way, through off-color remarks or jokes – it's not the buildings or the institution we call Happy State Bank; it is people within, Directors, Officers and Staff – everyone wants to be appreciated and respected

Stay quick and nimble – yet make long-term decisions – we can react to a customer's request/ emergency or a new expansion opportunity faster than any other competitor – we have to stay "quick on our feet" – we're also in this for the long haul – relationships are lasting – profits are only good if they are better than last month or last year – don't ever make a short-term decision that might make us a little money today when we can make a better long-term decision that makes us lots of money in the long run – being quick with a response while making a good long-term decision builds lasting relationships – and in the "heat of the battle," sometimes you have to make a tough decision by yourself…KNOW that the bank will stand with you and back you up – you are paid to make good judgment calls

Seek input, share everything, hide nothing, ask questions – we call it honest, professional adversarial- ism – we have a lot of smart people here – seek advice from lots of folks – and it's good to ask lots of questions – and don't take those questions personally – and don't be mean-spirited when asking questions – honesty and forthrightness always work – always make time and have time to talk to your co-workers – remem- ber, we are all on the same team working toward the same goals – the Bible says you should always "speak the truth with love"

TALK to each other – communication – if people would just talk to each other – talk in person first – via phone second – please use email as a last resort – it's hard to tell someone "no" or to be tacky when they are standing in front of you

Sometimes we make a mistake – admit it & fix it – FAST – it happens – get over it – everyone makes mistakes – and unless you make the same mistake over and over and over, mistakes are quickly forgiven here – the greater sin is to know a mistake was made and to not admit it or fix it – and when you make a mistake, don't compound it by making excuses – and it helps to say "I'm sorry" – the faster that you tell a customer (or co-worker) that you are sincerely sorry and you fix it (even make it better), the longer you will have that customer/co-worker

Give back – get involved in your community – it's considered part of your job at this bank – we meet lots of new people and hear of new banking opportunities when we are out and about – it makes you more valuable to the bank, which usually amounts to your paycheck looking better too – it also feels good when you get involved in projects that provide for a greater good

PRODUCE, DAMN IT (sometimes known as PDI!) – we expect excellence – we expect lots of quality **and** quantity at the same time – do it all – DO IT ALL – **DO IT ALL** – we believe that everyone who works here is a superstar – it takes every person doing their part, their job, to make this place run right and profitably every day – the bank gives a lot, and it expects a lot – the bottom line is still the bottom line – get rid of those who aren't producing and pulling their own weight

Laugh at work – most of us were born handsome (or pretty) instead of rich, and therefore we have to work for a living – but dang it, let's have fun – let's tell jokes – let's share funny emails – let's make fun of each other – all with respect of course – remember the "don't make anyone uncomfortable" deal – but dang it, let's laugh – the louder the better – and it is encouraged by management – you will be fired if you don't laugh

Every job is your job – there's no such thing as "not my job" – don't be haughty or pretentious – there is no such thing as a job that is "beneath" you – show that servant's heart

Don't watch the clock – the bank doesn't; you shouldn't either – this bank is great at giving folks (especially officers) lots of time off – whether it's for fun, family or sickness, we are quick and cheerful in letting you take time that you need – there are also times when this bank needs you to "burn some midnight oil" to get your job done and meet deadlines – no officer has EVER been told that they have taken too much time off or vacation – this ain't the place for 8 to 5ers – but there are also several who spend too much time at the bank and you need to find balance with your family – the key is balance – don't take advantage of the bank because the bank will not take advantage of you

Don't ever forget that it's OPM (OTHER PEOPLE'S MONEY) – we are trusted by our customers with their money – we are trusted by our stockholders with their investment dollars – and every now and then we have to work with customers to live up to their end of the deal – we have to collect past dues, overdrafts and fees – that's our job – we're giving our customers the opportunity to do the right thing – it is righteous work that we do – we must first use care and compassion, but every now and then we have to resort to other means (always legal) to collect – we want to be known as the "first bank you want to borrow from, but the last bank you want to owe" – never forget that it's OPM

Integrity, character, our reputation is everything -- DO WHAT'S RIGHT – always, every time, any time, no matter what it costs – no matter who it offends – no matter the perceived consequence – encourage it – reward it – revere it – make it the mantle that we are known for – it is expected

Be an owner – not a manager – there is a vast difference between the two – owners take **all** factors into consideration, not what is just expedient, least costly, most profitable or seems right at the time – be an entrepreneur, looking for opportunities to cut costs or increase revenues, or just making this place a nicer and better place to work – managers usually make selfish decisions

As Pat pointed out to me in a recent interview, one of the most important things about a list of values like this is that it *must be easy for people to buy into.* "They're the kind of values that everybody likes to have," he said, "and that makes a difference. We're not saying hate your mama. We're not saying be mean to people. We're saying take care of your family first. We're saying produce, dammit. We're saying do the stuff that makes you good. Good people want to hear that, and they want to live that. Good people love to be good, and lousy people love to find ways to be lousy. Good people are at their best when they're around good people. And you know what? If someone doesn't fit in with your team after you both talk about the values, they need to leave very quick. If they don't fit in, you get rid of them."

THE POWER OF ATTITUDE

I tell our clients that it is vitally important to connect at least one of the values to the habit of maintaining a positive attitude, no matter what…and it is just as important to ensure that the leader's example on this score, both during and after these meetings, is a consistent one. This is the part of living the values (which is, we need to remember, one of the core commitments) that often carries a learning curve—not just for the senior leader, but for every leader and indeed every employee in the organization. Attitude is everything. As Pat Hickman puts it:

"When it comes to those personality traits we want to see in people, the one that matters most is the one that shows up in the leader, and it's the ability to set aside a bad mood. As a leader, I'm not allowed a bad mood. It is off limits. If I come in in a lousy mood, it is a license to kill for every other person in this company. You can talk to my employees. They've seen me cry. They've seen me laugh. They've seen me jumping up and down with excitement. And yes, they've seen me angry. They've seen every emotion in the world. But they have never seen me in a bad mood. They've never seen me carry a black cloud around with me from room to room and meeting to meeting. I'm going to be positive every day all day, every time. My attitude always has to be *we're going to get through this.*

"That's the way it is for a leader. You've got to be the rock. Your positive attitude has got to be something people can depend on in good times and bad. I can honestly say to myself that in 32 years of running this company, you didn't see me in a bad mood. Now, *before* Happy State Bank, I made that mistake of letting a bad mood affect me and affect my relationships with other people. While I was still learning the ropes about how to lead, I did have some of those horrible mood swings, and guess what? It was a disrupter to the whole company I was working for. I realized it was just too expensive. It sabotaged everything."

This is one of the most important takeaways I highlight for leaders who are defining their values. Once you have defined them, do not undo all of your hard work up to this point and do not sabotage your organization by letting a bad mood get the better of you! Live the values in your own world every day, with a positive attitude—no matter what. Show people what that looks like. *Inspire* them to live the values in the same way in their world.

Chapter 6

Organizational Values Are Not Something We Create

VINCE LUBBEN is president and co-owner of Wireless World, an authorized Verizon retailer headquartered in Sioux Falls, South Dakota. Years ago, Vince heard me speak on accountability and asked me to come in and work with him and his employees on refining the company values. Although Wireless World had already done quite a bit of work on its organizational values and had circulated them widely, Vince set all that work aside while I led him and his team through the DEFINE process I have shared with you in this section. In other words, Vince did the right thing when he realized that the culture was not yet where he wanted it to be. He started from scratch because he realized how important this was.

Reviewing our work with Vince reminded me of one of the most important principles of the DEFINE step: Organizational values are not something we create. They are something we discover.

Organizational values are not something we create. They are something we discover.

The values are already there, waiting for us to recognize them and put them into words. They are in play whenever our people and our organization are living up to their true potential; they just might not have been defined properly and codified within the organization.

As a result of implementing the same process I have been sharing with you, Vince and his team identified and modeled the following powerful Wireless World values:

WIRELESS WORLD CORE VALUES

This is what we believe:

Customer Experience Is Everything We Are

Good or bad, our customers' perception defines us. Have Passion. Passion is Priceless.

Be Careful Stewards

Responsibly manage Wireless World co-workers and customer relationships, assets and reputation.

Adapt

Be creative in your thinking. Concentrate on the "cans," not the "can nots." Focus on the controllables and change quickly!

Serve the Community

Actively volunteer, give and participate in your community.

Communicate Clearly

Listen first, speak second. Design clearly defined goals. Be clear, even in uncertainty.

Be Accountable

Keep your commitments. Follow through on assigned responsibilities. Admit your mistakes and fix them fast.

Produce

Get your job done with excellence. Work hard and work smart. Succeed as a company and as an individual. Have a drive to win.

Grow & Develop

Pursue personal growth. Educate yourself and others. Read books. Learn from your faults.

Be Respectful

Follow the Golden Rule: Do unto others as you would have them do unto you.

Have an Attitude of Gratitude

Be gracious and appreciate what you have. Attitudes are contagious; pick a good one each morning.

Encourage Work/Life Balance

Work hard. Play hard.

You Are Valued

Team members are an essential piece to our success. Everyone has a voice. Everyone is heard. We are bigger than the sum of all of our parts.

Have Fun

Have a positive attitude. Find enthusiasm in your workplace...we hope it's at Wireless World.

Note that a brief, compelling *narrative* supports each of the Wireless World values and that its list of values checks all four of the boxes necessary for a great set of values: *foundational, professional, relational,* and *community*. Never forget: If you do not have a narrative and you have not touched all four of those bases, you do not yet have a strong value set!

After having defined, modeled, taught, protected, and celebrated these values, Vince was kind enough to send us the following quote to post on our website:

> "Employee turnover in our industry is very high. Our turnover last year was 32% but two other major companies in our industry had turnover of 100% and 300% respectively. I credit our lower turnover to the quality of the organizational culture that we created by working with Sam Silverstein."
>
> —Vince Lubben

Recently, I had the chance to catch up with Vince and see how things were going for him and his team. What follows are the highlights from that conversation.

So have those values we developed together with your team stayed relevant to Wireless World?

Absolutely. They're still key to our everyday life.

How do you know that?

We have sixty stores, and every one of those stores has a manager who lives the values. And we give them a lot of autonomy, but a lot of our store managers choose to reinforce the values verbally during their team meetings. Most of the district managers do as well. They ask someone on the team to pick a core value from the list, and then they talk about it as a group. And we talk about the values regularly during our weekly leadership meetings. You've got to talk about the values all the time; that's one of the big things I learned. More important, though, is that you've got to live them every day. That's certainly our aim.

How has defining the organizational values impacted your bottom line?

First and foremost, by reducing turnover. As you know, compared to the rest of our industry, our turnover numbers are extremely low— about one-third of the industry average. That's huge because lower turnover increases our profitability. It costs us about $10,000 to find somebody, interview them, onboard them, train them, and get them up to speed. So the better we are at doing that and the less often we have to do it, the better the bottom line is. And the work we did with you on defining our values has definitely been part of that success story.

How do you use your values with regard to hiring and onboarding new people?

Our values are an integral part of the new hire training. That's one of the first things people go over, and the values are featured prominently in the first pages of the new hire book we give people when they come on board. And of course, the managers are always looking for evidence of the values in people's lives and backgrounds when they do the interviewing, though that's done on an informal basis. When we bring someone new on board, we want to make sure they get how we operate, and that comes down to living the values. For instance, we love people who are competitive, but we also want people who understand that being No. 1 doesn't mean you push down the competition;

it just means you are totally committed to the values. It means you want to be the absolute best you can be in each of those areas. So, for example, with regard to *Guest Experience Is No. 1,* we want people who will strive to be No. 1 *for the guests.* We want people who will think, *Hey, I have an opportunity to improve lives this morning, even if it's just something small like helping a guest get their Facebook account set up on their phone.*

What some companies call "customers," you call "guests."

Yes, that's another important part of the value set. These are our guests, and we treat them that way.

What about the other side of the equation? Do you ever let people go because there's evidence that they aren't committed to living the values?

Absolutely. In fact, that's one of the big logistical advantages to having a clear set of values that everyone needs to buy into in order to contribute and be part of the team. It becomes very obvious when someone simply doesn't belong. You know, a few years ago, one of my district managers told me, "It's so much easier now to write somebody up or even fire them than it was before, because I can just say, 'Hey here's a core value that we live by. This is something we believe in and are committed to here at Wireless World, and you're not living that value, so that's why you're getting this write-up.' Or even: 'That's why we're letting you go,' if there's a clear pattern of refusing to live the value. There's no debate." That's a huge advantage compared to before we worked with you, Sam. When you try to quote policies at people, it's easy to get lost in the employee manual. But when there is a clear list of values that everyone knows about and can see people living by, you don't get the long, drawn-out arguments. People understand when there's not a good fit, and they either change or they move on and find something else to do. That's what happens when you define a strong set of values.

Wireless World's experience is not unique. Much larger organizations have followed the same process and reached the same conclusion about the importance of the right set of values. As Ron Mittelstaedt, CEO of Waste Connections, put it: "Unless you consciously design the right set of organizational values, you will eventually fail. Without a clear set of values that you all live, each and every day, you have a zero percent chance of success. I think they're absolutely critical."

TO TROUBLESHOOT THE DEFINE STEP... CHECK THE MIRROR

If the leader has worked with the team to identify a great set of values and people are not yet living and reaching those values, there are only two possible reasons for that:

- clarity is missing because something covered in this DEFINE section of the book has not yet been executed,

Or

- the values are not yet being modeled, taught, protected, or celebrated.

Remember: Our values are not an exercise in public relations; they are what we believe and how we operate. They are the means by which we create a sustainable competitive advantage! They are the key to a high-performance culture, so defining them clearly is something that is worth getting right.

"Open your arms to change, but don't let go of your values." —the Dalai Lama

If you have made it this far in the book, I am assuming that you are committed not just to completing the DEFINE step but to working the entire Accountability Advantage™ process. That means your next job is making sure leadership is setting the right example. Once the values and the commitments are clear, you will want to look very closely at the next step in creating a high-performance culture that people want to be a part of: *modeling it from the top.*

III

Model the
CULTURE

Chapter 7

We Get What We Give

WHEN IT COMES TO ACCOUNTABILITY, we get only what we give.

As I noted earlier in this book, accountability can never be mandated; it can only be inspired. That means that if leaders do not model accountability, it will not become part of the organizational culture. Period.

If we as leaders want to model accountability for others, we must be able to answer this question whenever, wherever, and however it arises: *What is accountability?*

How do you answer that question?

We have asked this question of tens of thousands of leaders at organizations all around the world. We have heard thousands of answers in response. And I have personally consulted more dictionaries, white papers, and business school textbooks than I care to calculate in search of the best, most practical definition. I have never found an answer to this essential question better than this one:

Accountability is keeping your commitments to people.

> **Accountability is keeping your commitments to people.**

That is it. That is what accountability means. If we can just keep our eye on that definition, we will be in a position to model accountability—and thereby transform our relationships, our teams, our organization, and, eventually, the community and the world in which we live. Once we grasp this definition and commit to live by it, we can use accountability to create massive, measurable improvements in all of those realms of life. How? By keeping our relational commitments, meaning our commitments to people that support the relationship… and thereby inspiring them to become more accountable.

> **"A good objective of leadership is to help those who are doing poorly to do well, and to help those who are doing well to do even better."**
> —Jim Rohn

FOUR POWERFUL WORDS

For leaders, the conversation about modeling an accountable working culture can always be boiled down to four powerful words: *accountability starts with us.*

Do we want our people to tell us the truth? Then we as leaders must first make a commitment to the truth.

Do we want our people to act with integrity? Then we as leaders must first make a commitment to identify what we value, tell the story of our values, and then live what we value.

Do we want our people to think and act like a team? Then we as leaders must first make a commitment to "It's all of us."

Do we want our people to respond loyally, effectively, and resourcefully when times are tough? Then we as leaders must first make a commitment to stand with our people when all hell breaks loose.

Do we want our low-level and mid-level performers to become top performers, and do we want our top performers to stick around? Then we as leaders must first make a commitment to the faults and failures, as well as the opportunities and successes.

Do we want our people to use the organization's resources responsibly? Then we as leaders must first make a commitment to sound financial principles.

Do we want our team and our organization to achieve at the highest level of which it is capable? Then we as leaders must make a commitment to helping individuals reach their potential and be their best.

Do we want our people to treat customers well—so well that they want to come back for more and tell others to do business with us? Then we as leaders must make a commitment to a physically and emotionally safe environment for our people.

Do we want our people to move heaven and earth to keep their commitments to us and tell us well in advance when they face an unexpected obstacle that keeps them from doing what they said they would do? Then we as leaders must make a commitment to make our word our bond.

Do we want our people to show up inspired and proud to work for our organization? Then we as leaders must make a commitment to a good reputation.

So we have to stop thinking about holding someone else accountable. That is the big shift. As leaders, we want to move this discussion to the next level, the level of *helping* our people be accountable by *modeling* that accountability first. This is how leaders inspire accountability in others.

DOES THE *SENIOR* LEADER LIVE THE VALUES AND KEEP THE COMMITMENTS?

The second step, Model the Culture, is all about *leaders* living the values and keeping the commitments, even when doing so means having a difficult conversation or making a decision that takes them out of their comfort zone. That starts with the leader at the top. It is great when all the leaders in the organization live the values and keep the commitments. In fact, that is the best-case scenario. But it is important that we stop and notice that step two of the Accountability Advantage™ process, Model the Culture, is never taking place *unless* the most senior leader is living the values and keeping the commitments.

> Step two of the Accountability Advantage™ process, Model the Culture, is never taking place unless the most senior leader is living the values and keeping the commitments.

This reality brings us to an interesting discussion about the organizational dynamics that immediately follow the completion of step one, Define the Culture.

"IS THIS FOR REAL?"

Once you discover, codify, and communicate the values, something fascinating happens within the organization. People start to watch the senior leader with much more attention and interest than usual.

Why is that? Because people want to figure out whether the values the leader has been talking about lately are for real. Does the leader really believe these values…or is this simply an exercise in "motivation" that will be replaced with another such exercise next month, next year, or next quarter?

If the leader really believes the values, that they are important, and that they are non-negotiable, meaning that we will always live them, then the leader's actions, aligning with the values, will demonstrate all of that immediately. If that happens, people will change their patterns of belief and action by following the leader's example and living the values.

On the other hand, if people decide the leader *does not* believe in and act on the values, they will slip back into a (possibly toxic or dysfunctional) working culture by default. It is that simple. People do not want to be involved in a "flavor of the week" exercise. They want to be a part of a positive, transformational, and permanent change.

This is a critical part of cultural growth that leaders often overlook. It is not enough to define the values. The team must see tangible evidence *from the top* that the values really are driving beliefs, actions, and decisions.

Think of the modeling step as being like one of those old-fashioned rows of Christmas tree lights with removable colored bulbs that people used to use decades ago. You know the kind I mean. When one of the lights went out, the entire row of lights went dark. The senior leader is basically the very first light on that string of lights. If he or she is not living the values, the values will instantly go dark everywhere. It is the leader's job to turn that first light on and make sure it shines brightly—and the sooner the better.

And when we say "the sooner the better," we mean it. In fact, in our experience, organizations that successfully define a strong value set must *immediately* prove to the rest of the organization that the values are *for real.* They do that by making tough decisions that *prove* those values are real.

Let me share a common scenario that often plays out as the "moment of truth" for a leader who has worked hard with the team to discover and codify a powerful set of organizational values. Here is what happens.

Let's say that there are 100 people working within the organization, which we will call Acme Corporation. Of those 100 people, let's say 90 are on board with the newly codified list of organizational values. Ninety people are looking forward to living and working in an environment where those values really are "the way we do things around here."

That is good news, right? Ninety people out of 100? Well, yes and no. Ninety is definitely moving in the right direction...but those ten people represent a special challenge for the leader. And if the leader is going to deliver on the goal of modeling the values that support the working culture, *that modeling has to happen right away.*

There are only two ways this scenario can play out following the circulation of the values that have been discovered and refined. We call the first way it can play out the *cultural death spiral.*

THE "CULTURAL DEATH SPIRAL" SCENARIO

There are some people at Acme Corporation who are *unaligned* with the values that the CEO, Jane Acme, worked so hard with her employees to discover and refine. These people—the so-called "bad apples"—are making decisions that *do not* align with the values. They do not say out loud that they disagree with the values, of course, but their actions have a way of speaking louder than their words. One of those people, Bill Hotshot, is the top-producing salesperson in the company.

Now, one of the values Jane and her team put on the list is:

Be respectful.

Another is:

Tell the truth.

Bill Hotshot has nodded his head obediently and even spoken up in support of these values during team meetings...but four days after the values list is shared and explained, Jane notices disturbing signs that Bill is not living the values. Indeed, Bill has for years had a challenge when it comes to respecting colleagues—and even, on occasion, respecting customers.

The most recent examples of this—the ones that Jane can confirm with certainty have happened over the past four days—are:

- Bill told Lauren, a fellow employee who works in Accounting, to "shut up and get back to counting beans" when Lauren asked him when he would be filing his monthly expense report. He laughed after this remark, but Lauren did not think it was funny and asked for an apology. She did not get one.

- Bill used the company email system to send a sexist joke and an inappropriate picture to his manager, Yolanda. She did not find it amusing.

- Bill was heard saying to a colleague that Brenda, who works in Reception, was "dumb as a post, like most receptionists." The next day, he denied making the remark, although four people heard it.

Again: Jane has absolute certainty that all of these events happened *after* Bill agreed to live the Acme values. The instant she hears about and confirms these events, she faces an Accountability Moment of Truth. Jane chooses to disengage. She fails the test. (Jane has a history of not stepping up at such moments, which is problematic, but now there is no grey area. She is not living the values.)

When Lauren, the employee who works in Accounting, requests a private meeting with Jane to share her concerns about the way Bill is interacting with others, Jane thinks for a moment and then says, "Bill is an emotional guy, but he's a good salesperson. I've talked with Yolanda, and we both agree that it would be difficult or impossible to replace Bill in either the short or the long term. I'll be sure to talk to him about this personally, though."

This was another Accountability Moment of Truth. Jane fails this one, too. She does not talk to Bill personally about what happened. After the meeting with Lauren, she sends Bill a vaguely worded email reminding him how important it is to live the values—but without referencing any of the specific actions he took that were not in alignment with the values *Be respectful* and *Tell the truth*. And she does not outline any consequences for continuing to ignore these values. By chickening out, Jane lets down Lauren, Yolanda, and the whole team.

Bill's pattern of disrespectful behavior and deception continues. And still there are no consequences.

By the end of the month, no one in the organization is making an effort to live the values. No one is even bothering to think about them.

This was an Accountability Moment of Truth, too. And Jane, the CEO, failed it. She did not defend the value *Be respectful,* and she did not live the value *Tell the truth* because she told Lauren she would talk to Bill about his behavior in person—and then she did not do that.

As a result of Jane's choices (not Bill's! Bill is not the senior leader!), the culture slipped back into default mode. And all the good work people had put into the values was undone. Everything her team did in step one was a complete waste of time. Jane lost credibility. Every time she started to talk about accountability, people nodded obediently… and tuned her out.

That is the death spiral scenario.

Now, let's take a look at the *accountable scenario.*

THE ACCOUNTABLE SCENARIO

All the same things happen—up until the point when Jane promises Lauren, on day four, that she will talk to Bill personally. Jane keeps that promise.

She sits down privately with both Bill and his supervisor, Yolanda, and reviews in detail exactly what happened and why each of Bill's choices did not align with the values.

Jane asks Bill directly whether he wants to keep working at Acme (he says he does) and reminds him that if he wants to be part of the team, he needs to live the values.

Jane asks Yolanda, Bill's manager, to work daily with Bill for 15 minutes, in private, on what it looks like to live the values, specifically the values of *Being respectful* and *Telling the truth*. Both Yolanda and Bill agree to do this work together.

On day eight, Jane gets another report, confirmed by multiple employees, that Bill has again told Lauren in Accounting to "shut up and get back to counting beans." When she confirms that this is in fact what took place, she instructs Yolanda to terminate Bill.

Top salesperson or no top salesperson, Jane decides that the values come first. Bill will need to find some other organization where he can interact in the way he prefers to interact with people. He cannot work at Acme.

In the days and weeks that follow, multiple employees tell Jane how glad they are she let Bill go. Morale—and performance—improve everywhere, including on the sales team. By the way, the sales team beats quota.

So here is the critical question: Do the actions of the leader support the values, even when it's not easy?

> Do the actions of the leader support
> the values, even when it's not easy?

All too often, the answer is no. And the reason is simple: there is a courage deficit. That sounds harsh, but it is not meant to be. It is just reality. Courage does not happen overnight. It takes time to build up courage in a difficult situation. That is true for everyone, and it is certainly true for leaders who are working on their culture.

STRENGTHENING THE COURAGE MUSCLE

Many leaders fail to prepare themselves for the reality that modeling the values they have just worked so hard with the team to discover will take significant reservoirs of personal courage. But it does.

When we define the values and the relational commitments, we may not always realize that supporting them comes at a price. If we are serious about modeling the values, fulfilling the commitments, and building an accountable culture, we have to be willing to pay that price. We have to be ready to have some difficult conversations and make some difficult choices. And if that is not something we have built up enough practice doing as leaders, we are going to want to arrange for support from a coach, a consultant, or a peer group. Leaders sometimes need that kind of relationship to help them become comfortable with the idea that they have a right and a responsibility to set and protect a standard in the organization when it comes to living the organizational values.

> If you are a leader, you have a right and a responsibility to set and protect a standard when it comes to living the organizational values.

Sometimes this is a new way for a leader to understand their authority, their accountability, and their leadership position. When that is the case, the leader may need a little help making living the values second nature. It is a sign of strength to acknowledge that need and then to take action to address it.

Here are three powerful reasons it makes sense for leaders to get the coaching and support they need so they are prepared to step up and move beyond their comfort zone in the period immediately following the Define the Culture step.

Reason #1: As leaders, we may get too used to accommodating certain people. This is natural, and in some circumstances, it is even praiseworthy. After all, it is important to be able to listen without judgment, to compromise when appropriate, and to see the positive aspects of a team member's personality. *But never at the expense of the values!* If we are making excuses for a "key person" because of that person's connections, capacity to bring in revenue, seniority, or for any other reason, the accommodation habit is harming the culture the moment it results in someone—anyone—ignoring the values.

How do you know if the accommodation habit has compromised your team, your organization, and your working culture? Here is one of the most common signs: you come up with creative euphemisms that whitewash the behavior and decisions of someone who is not living the values. So, for instance, if one of your values is *Respect*, but Bill is not aligning with that value and is not responding to coaching meant to help him learn to align with that value, do you say anything like this to other people in the organization when you are talking about Bill?

- "Bill is an emotional guy."
- "Bill is old-school." (Or, just as common: "Bill is part of the younger generation.")
- "Bill has a lot on his plate."
- "Bill knows a lot about this business."
- "Bill has a great network of contacts."
- "Bill shoots his mouth off—just ignore him when he does that."
- "Bill didn't mean anything by that."
- "That's just Bill."

And so on. You get the idea. Bill may very well be emotional, he may be 65 (or 25), he may have an overloaded schedule, he may know a lot, and he may have hundreds of cool social media connections. All of those things may very well be true, but *none of them is a reason to stop the conversation about whether Bill's actions and decisions align with the values.* If they do not, Bill needs coaching and support. If Bill does not respond to that coaching and support, there needs to be consequences, up to and including the possibility of termination.

Reason #2: As leaders, we may have a knee-jerk fear that we will not be able to fill open positions. Sometimes this fear is rooted in a leader's lack of familiarity with the basics of recruitment, interviewing, onboarding, and retention. Sometimes it is rooted in an unhealthy desire to avoid admitting we have made a mistake in hiring someone or in allowing someone to be hired. And sometimes this fear is simple worst-case-scenario thinking: We read a few headlines about a tight labor market or a challenge that people in some other company or industry are having in filling a certain kind of position, and we assume that the same problem will bring our own business to a standstill. Or we may just not like taking on the perceived risk of filling a position with someone we don't know. In all of these situations, we opt to stick with troubles we know about rather than opening ourselves up to new possibilities, new relationships, and new levels of creativity and expertise. When the "troubles we know about" are people who refuse to live the values, we sabotage our own organizational culture and our organization's potential by keeping them on. We need to move past that fear and replace the person with someone who can live the values. Make no mistake: this is an Accountability Moment of Truth.

Very often, we fail that test because we have grown used to selling ourselves excuses that justify unaccountable behavior—and then selling the excuses to others in the organization. In this case, the excuses tend to sound like this:

- "Well, the devil you know is better than the devil you don't."
- "At least, with Bill, we know what we've got."
- "You play the hand you're dealt."

We cannot model the culture we want…and at the same time sell ourselves excuses about why it is okay not to live the values.

> We cannot model the culture we want…and at the same time sell ourselves excuses about why it is okay not to live the values.

When, as leaders, we start talking ourselves out of living the values, it goes without saying that we are not *modeling* those values. Instead, what we are modeling in these moments is the decision to *abandon* the values, and that is a failure of leadership.

Let's be honest with ourselves here. If, instead of taking action, a doctor made excuses in order to get around a problem they had a clear responsibility to address, we would apply a word to that behavior: *malpractice*. As leaders, we need to accept the reality that we can commit leadership malpractice. How do we do it? By selling ourselves excuses and trying to sell those excuses to others…when we really do know better. When we do that, we are the equivalent of a doctor examining a patient with a textbook case of appendicitis and saying, "Well, it's true, we are looking at appendicitis, and it could kill you if we do nothing, but at least we know what it is. So let's not rock the boat by talking about surgery, because that would mean I have to go outside of my comfort zone." We would not accept that kind of response from a physician, and we should not accept it from ourselves as leaders. There are risks to surgery, of course, but the risks of taking no action far outweigh the risk of removing the appendix. By the same token, there are risks to letting someone go who refuses to live the values, but the risks of letting them stay and destroy the culture are far greater.

Notice the excuses you try to sell yourself. Acknowledge that they *are* excuses. Then give yourself a reality check. So, for instance: *The devil you know is not better than the devil you don't.* We do not know who is a "devil" and who is not until we have the experience of working with the person. Pretending otherwise is a lie—an excuse—that keeps us from modeling our values.

By the same token: *The fact that we know what we've got with Bill is a marker of our personal accountability, not a reason not to take action in a way that aligns with our values.* When we, as the leader, know there is a problem, we have to honor our commitments to those who follow us to fix that problem. So, what do we do? We fix it, of course.

Last but not least: *Playing the hand we're dealt is not necessarily the right response, and it certainly is not the right philosophy for living our lives.* The "play the hand you're dealt" excuse conveniently ignores the reality that as leaders, *we* are the ones who can shuffle the deck and start a new deal anytime we choose. It is our team. It is our deck. We need to own that.

Whenever we run into leaders who are so afraid of finding the right people in a tough market that they sell themselves excuses like these, we urge them to consider the companies we have seen and worked with who have long, long lists of applicants *whenever* an opening appears, *regardless* of what is happening in the labor market. We can create an organization that attracts the best and the brightest, even in a zero-unemployment environment, and we can do that without breaking the bank.

By the way: My experience is that organizations with an accountable working culture offer pay packages that are industry-competitive but not absurd. Companies that offer those high-end compensation packages are, very often, doing that because it is the only way for them to attract the most talented people. Guess what? The moment someone comes along with a slightly higher compensation package, that team member is gone. Why? Because the loyalty of team members is a function of an accountable organizational culture! We have to build an organization that attracts and retains the very best people. And modeling the values that support an accountable culture is the only way to do that.

> The loyalty of team members is a function of having an accountable organizational culture.

Reason #3: We are fixated on a certain short-term outcome. If we are thinking more about whether the sales team will hit a monthly quota than we are about whether the organization as a whole is living the kind of culture that attracts the best and the brightest, our priorities are misplaced. Period. And P.S., by building the kind of organization that people want to work at, encourage others in their circle to work at, and will do anything within their power and their value set to *keep* working at, we make it far more likely for the sales team, and everyone else, to establish new and higher goals and create new and higher levels of performance to match.

Yes, it takes courage to act in support of the stated values, but what is the alternative? A deeper and deeper sinkhole of a culture by default. When we make excuses for Bill, when we tell ourselves how hard it is going to be to replace Bill, when we think about Bill's impact on the monthly quota but ignore his impact on the morale of the organization as a whole, *we are sabotaging the team.* We are creating a self-fulfilling prophecy of subpar performance and validating a mediocre working culture. And that is not okay. We must live the values. We must set the example. As Pat Hickman of Happy State Bank puts it:

"Here's what it boils down to. You may be able to get away with it at home when you say, 'Don't do what I do; do what I say. But you can't get away with that in the workplace if you're a leader.

"You know, the first leadership course I ever took, I think I was 14 or 15 years old. It was in 1967, and it happened at a boy scout camp. We all made this big wood plaque with a wood burner, and the three words on it, written in huge letters, were SET THE EXAMPLE.

"Those were the first three words I learned as a leader. And I can't tell you how many times I've thought of them over the course of my career. If I show up late, everybody else is going to show up late. If I come in sloppily dressed, everybody else is going to do that. Once you're a leader, you're setting the example in all that you do. That's the best possible way to model the values and the culture and the quality of the work you expect. Set the example. If you're expecting excellence out of your own actions and decisions, you are going to be in a much better position to expect excellence out of everybody else."

Pat is absolutely right. And as we will see in chapter 8, the time to expect excellence out of our own actions and decisions is *right now...* because the cultural clock begins ticking the instant we complete the Defining the Culture step and move into Modeling the Culture.

Chapter 8

The Clock Is Ticking

WE ALWAYS TELL LEADERS: "YOUR CULTURE'S CLOCK IS TICKING. That means you can expect an Accountability Moment of Truth during the FIRST WEEK after you start telling the story of your values. In fact, you can expect a couple of Moments of Truth!"

The way the leader responds to those Moments of Truth will have a huge impact on whether the stated values take root and begin to guide the organization's thinking and behavior. I cannot overemphasize the importance of modeling the values, prominently and publicly, even when it hurts, during that first critical week. The reason for this is simple: Bad news travels fast. So if we, as leaders, miss out on an opportunity to model the values, we cannot be surprised when people in our organization start talking about that failure!

A failure of senior leadership to pass the Accountability Moments of Truth that arise in the week immediately after leadership starts telling the story of the organizational values sabotages the culture. In fact, it does so more effectively than any disaffected team member.

> A failure of senior leadership to pass the Accountability Moments of Truth that arise in the week immediately after leadership starts telling the story of the organizational values sabotages the culture. In fact, it does so more effectively than any disaffected team member can.

The way leaders show up personally in terms of living the values right after they have led the team through the Define the Culture step is all-important. If the leader's decisions and actions fail to align with what people have just agreed to, credibility and buy-in go out the window. People say things to themselves and to each other like the following:

- "Jane's not serious about what she said about values the other day."
- "Jane is all about respect and telling the truth—unless she's talking to someone in our department."
- "What do you expect with Jane's management? She talks a good game, but when push comes to shove, she doesn't respect us and she doesn't feel she has to tell us the truth. All she respects is the almighty dollar."

And the culture is right back to default. Jane may not hear this kind of thing first-hand when she talks to people one on one or makes a visit to the break room. But if she fails even one of the Accountability Moment of Truth tests during that critical first week, she can be certain the conversations are happening, both in person and digitally.

It may sound like we are saying that leaders need to be perfect during the critical first few days following the Define the Culture step. But of course, that's impossible. We all make mistakes. We all lose sight of the values from time to time. We all make choices that do not align with our stated values. That happens daily, *even at organizations with a high-performance working culture,* the kind of culture that makes people glad they work at that organization and eager to keep working there. But there is a difference at organizations with an accountable working culture. At those kinds of organizations, the moment someone *realizes* they have lost sight of one of the values, they instantly acknowledge what has happened. Then they take action to fix the problem in a way that reclaims that value!

> Whenever you lose sight of the values, openly acknowledge what happened, then fix it and fix it fast.

When you lose sight of the values, openly acknowledge what happened, then fix it and fix it fast. This is the behavior that leaders need to master; and frankly, it is the one with which they sometimes need help in the days following the completion of the Define the Culture step.

When we openly acknowledge that we have acted out of alignment with the values, when we do not pretend that all of our decisions are perfect, when we quickly take action to fix what happened, fix it openly, and fix it fast, then the team knows that we are serious. They know that we are willing to live the values, even when it is inconvenient. They know that when push comes to shove, the values come first.

You may recall that one of Happy State Bank's core values is the following:

> **Attitude is everything** – Life is 10% what happens to you and 90% your attitude toward it. Give your heart, not just your words and/or your actions. Co-owners

and customers can see through poor and lousy attitudes or insincerity – a good attitude is OK, but a great attitude is expected – don't let good take the place of great – be the best person that you can be

Pat Hickman told me: "I wish I could tell you I've never violated that value. I wish I could tell you I've never gotten angry. I have. But I do want to tell you that I knew about it every time it happened, and I went about fixing it. It didn't happen often, but when it did, within two days I was back in that person's office face to face asking for their forgiveness. That's an important conversation. I had to let them know that I realized I overstepped my bounds, that we can't act the way I acted when I got angry, that I was sorry, that I lost my temper and I should not have said what I said in the way I said it, and please, please forgive me so we can start all over."

This is what "fixing it" looks like and sounds like. This is what leaders in high-performance organizations learn to do.

> "Integrity: The choice between what's convenient and what's right."
>
> —Tony Dungy

Making a mistake that takes us out of alignment with the values *and then quickly taking action to fix that mistake*, publicly and without trying to justify our mistake, is one of the very best ways to model the values. This kind of action sticks with people, and it lets them know where we stand, both as leaders and as human beings.

Consider once again the cultural death spiral scenario—and then imagine what would have happened if Jane had taken this approach *right after* she first realized that she had acted out of alignment with the stated values.

The moment Jane realized she had failed to take action in defense of the values by not engaging when she confirmed that Bill was not living the values, she could have told Bill, his manager, and everyone on the sales team that this was a big problem, one she had mistakenly chosen to ignore. She could have said that ignoring this problem was not okay and that she did not want to build a company where people ignored such problems. She could have said that she would be working with Bill's manager to ensure that everyone on the sales team got the coaching and support they needed to get a clear understanding of the values and to live and work in alignment with them.

If Jane had done that right away—the second she realized that her decision to ignore the problem was out of alignment with the company's stated values—she could have righted the ship. Leaders always get the culture they deserve.

> **Leaders always get the culture they deserve.**

Values matter. As leaders, we must commit to identifying the right values, modeling the right values, and living the right values, whether or not anyone is looking. Period. It does not matter how pretty the stated values sound. What matters is the action we take and the choices we make.

MAKING MONEY IS NOT A VALUE!

When senior leadership sends, by word or by example, the message that anything is acceptable as long as it has a positive impact on the bottom line, values vanish and bad things start to happen.

Making money cannot be the only behavior the organization rewards. Money is like oxygen. Yes, human beings need oxygen in order to survive, but the purpose of a human life is not to breathe air. Our individual purpose needs to be rooted in some deeper aspiration. It is the same for an organization. If the purpose of our organization is just to make money, we are missing some important ingredients, notably contribution and integrity.

When the senior leader in an organization makes the decision that it is okay to cut corners, that it is okay to operate in a way that rewards only financial gain, that it is okay to lie if no one notices, what are they really telling everyone at the organization? They are saying that integrity does not matter in any decision, in any communication, or in any planning session. They are saying, "The problem with cutting corners is not that it goes against our values—the problem is getting caught."

This kind of "leadership" can carry devastating consequences. It creates an organization where the core operating principle sounds something like this: "I am here to make a buck. And you'd better watch your back, because if I can make a buck at your expense, it's no different from me making a buck at someone else's expense."

Does that sound like someplace where you would want to build your career? Does that sound like someplace that the best and brightest would actively seek out? Does it sound like the kind of place where the best and the brightest would choose to stay?

"The world is changed by your example, not by your opinion."

—Paulo Coelho

The working culture is *always* determined by the leader's personal commitments to the team. One of those commitments, you will recall, is identifying, defining, and living a powerful, positive set of values—the kind of values that are lived so consistently, and are seen as so integral to the identity of the organization and everyone who works for it, that the instant someone tries to cut corners, the culture kicks in automatically. When you are doing this right, someone sitting next to the person who is *about* to cut corners says, "Hey, that's not how we do things around here." If the values are there, if the leader has established them properly, that is what happens. People speak up. And if nobody speaks up, *that means the values are not being lived at the top.* So live them—and when you slip up, which you will, master the art of noticing that you slipped up and fixing that, fast.

Chapter 9

It's All Personal

CREATING AN ACCOUNTABLE workplace culture is not easy. If it were easy, most organizations would do it. Most organizations do *not* do it. Why not?

The No. 1 reason the majority of organizations do not define, sustain, and defend an accountable high-performance culture that people want to be a part of is a failure of leadership. Why does that failure happen?

The No. 1 reason we have seen that leaders fail in this area is that they themselves do not model the values. Why don't they model the values?

In our experience, the No. 1 reason leaders do not model the values is that they fall victim to a special brand of entitlement that I call the "Just Business" mindset. That mindset is what we will be looking at closely in this chapter.

"IT'S JUST BUSINESS"

If we lack courage as leaders, it is all too easy for us to cover that fact up. Whenever someone calls us out for not living the values (by, for instance, letting a senior salesperson stay on even though that salesperson refuses to live the values), we have an instant response that we can use to shut down the conversation. We can say, "Hey, it's not personal. It's just business. I just have to think of the bottom line. Bill is good at what he does, and I can't afford to lose him."

Nonsense. We *can* afford to lose Bill. What we cannot afford to lose is our organizational values. We have made a clear commitment to living those values. When we abandon that commitment, it affects people. By choosing not to model those values, we have *made* it personal for the rest of the organization. We have told them we care so little about the commitments we made to them that we are not willing to take a stand for those commitments. It is impossible for them not to take that personally! And we should not be surprised when they opt to follow our example and not keep their commitments to us.

Turning this (sadly common) syndrome around is a gut-check moment. As leaders, we may come up with all kinds of excuses for our failure to live the values, and we may defend those decisions with the "It's just business" defense. We may think we are committed to the values, but remember: commitment is *no matter what!*

> We may think we are committed to the values, but remember: commitment is *no matter what!*

Are we engaging in the kind of favoritism that undercuts the diversity, equity, and inclusion commitments we say we value? No problem. We can say: "It's nothing personal that you were not trained for that opportunity. This is just business." And the problem goes away.

Are we minimizing the human impact of a decision that negatively impacts the quality of life of our team members (for example, by redesigning the compensation plan in such a way that it reduces someone's income)? If someone has a problem with this, all we have to do is repeat the magic words: "It's nothing personal. This is just business." And we can keep on making short-term decisions that have disastrous long-term impacts.

A sidenote: You might be wondering, *Does this mean we cannot make decisions that are in the best interest of our business? Does this mean we cannot ever redesign a compensation plan or shut down a department?* Of course not. No one is saying that. What we are saying, though, is that as leaders, we must remind ourselves constantly that every decision we make is going to have a personal impact on someone. When we hire someone, we are taking on a personal relationship with that person. A leader is someone who makes commitments for the safety and well-being of the people around them and keeps those commitments. We need to think about how our decisions are likely to affect that relationship, both in the short term and the long term.

The accountable leader, the leader who builds a high-performance culture that is truly inspiring, always takes their people into account when they are making decisions. They work like crazy to make the kinds of decisions that are not going to put them in a position, a month or six months or two years down the road, of having to correct a mistake by making another decision that is going to have a negative impact on the team.

Accountable leaders never forget that their decisions affect people, and they do all they possibly can to ensure that those decisions will affect their team in a positive way. When they do have to make a decision that impacts their team in a negative way, they look for the outcome that allows them to take the best care of their people. Accountable leaders live by this standard: *make the best decisions you possibly can on the front end, think hard about each decision's impact on your people, and always protect your people to the best of your ability.* They know that every decision they make eventually intersects with someone else's life on a personal level.

Leaders at all levels need to understand—it is never just business; it is always personal. Any interaction between two human beings is, by definition, personal. Any decision that affects a relationship is, by definition, personal.

> It is never just business; it is always personal. Any interaction between two human beings is, by definition, personal. Any decision that affects a relationship is, by definition, personal.

Ron Mittelstaedt of Waste Connections put it this way: "People can get paid anywhere. They need to feel valued. They need to know they're appreciated. They need to know they're going to be cared for personally and professionally. They need to know that you've got their back. They need to know what they're doing matters, and they need to know what the organization is doing matters. Those are the things people care about. Money is important; you've got to be competitive. But just being competitive and paying them what they deserve—that's not why people stay. They stay because they feel they belong with you and your organization."

A PERSONAL RELATIONSHIP DESERVES RESPECT

Whether we realize it or not as leaders, we have a personal relationship with *everyone* we come in contact with. As in: every single individual—not just team members!

Sure, the members of our team have a personal relationship with us, but it does not stop there. The vendors we choose to work with have a personal relationship with us, too. The person we buy a cup of coffee from at Starbucks has a personal relationship with us. The relationship may be fleeting, but it is there, and if we pretend it does not exist, we are wrong.

Everybody we interact with has a personal relationship with us that is deserving of respect. If we choose to treat any one of those individuals—the team member, the vendor, the clerk at Starbucks—as a means to an end, if we pretend they are not part of the world our leadership and our life affects, then we sabotage the relationship. And when we do that, we sabotage the culture our leadership and our life connect to. Treating someone as a means to an end, pretending that doing this is "just business" so we do not have to make or keep a relational commitment, is like drilling a hole in our own boat. We can tell ourselves that it is only a little hole…but little holes matter. The water is still getting in and the boat is still going to sink if we do not plug the leaks. Again: We get the culture we deserve!

And when it comes to team members, the equation is pretty simple: if we expect our people to be accountable to us, we have to honor our commitments to them. We have to care for them, authentically, *as people* and not as means to an end. If we are not serious about caring for people *because they are people*, if what we really care about is the money and we see our relationships with people as a vehicle for making bottom-line outcomes happen, we cannot model an accountable culture! It is simply impossible.

DOES THE LEADER VALUE PEOPLE? HOW DO YOU KNOW?

Personal commitments matter.

That may seem like an obvious point. It is not. It requires constant reinforcement, especially within leadership circles. You would be surprised how many leaders we run into imagine that their commitments do not need to be personal. They say things like "I am committed to quality" or "I am committed to making this company No. 1 in its field." Yet somehow they never grasp the importance of making personal commitments to actual human beings.

So, let's be clear. Without a personal commitment, there is no accountability. Teams and organizations that struggle with sustaining good relationships also struggle with accountability. Without strong relationships, we cannot achieve anything of consequence, live up to our full potential, or make any kind of meaningful contribution as leaders or as human beings.

We are interconnected and interdependent, and our personal commitments matter. This principle holds true whether we are talking about a relationship that unfolds in our personal life or one that unfolds in our professional life. The kinds of commitments that support relationships are exactly the same in each realm.

Precisely the same rules apply whether you are the leader of a Fortune 1000 enterprise struggling to chart its path through an unprecedented economic downturn...or a member of a family struggling to stay sane and whole and safe in the midst of a global pandemic.

The rules of the game are identical in both situations. Accountable relationships require personal commitment in the ten areas I have already shared with you. Here they are again. They warrant repetition here because *these commitments are what leaders must model in the second step of this process!* Making and keeping these commitments is how people *know* that the leader authentically values people.

THE TEN NON-NEGOTIABLE RELATIONAL COMMITMENTS THAT CREATE ACCOUNTABILITY

A *relational commitment* is a commitment that serves a relationship with one or more people. The ten core relational commitments appear below. All are non-negotiable for accountable leaders.

I COMMIT TO HELPING INDIVIDUALS REACH THEIR POTENTIAL AND BE THEIR BEST. When my people know I care about their growth and development, they care about the organization's growth and development.

I COMMIT TO TRUTH. Lying and accountability cannot coexist.

I COMMIT TO LIVING THE VALUES. Our organization's non-negotiable core values state our shared principles and our standards of behavior.

I COMMIT TO "IT'S ALL OF US." I accept that if the other person fails, I fail, and I do not succeed unless the other person succeeds.

I COMMIT TO EMBRACING FAULTS AND FAILURES AS WELL AS OPPORTUNITIES AND SUCCESSES. I am not perfect, and I do not expect others to be perfect.

I COMMIT TO SOUND FINANCIAL PRINCIPLES. This commitment is all about stewardship and making wise decisions with our financial resources.

I COMMIT TO A SAFE SPACE. This commitment is about creating and sustaining an environment of physical, emotional, and psychological safety.

I COMMIT TO "MY WORD IS MY BOND." What we say must align with what we do. If I say it, people can depend on it.

I COMMIT TO STANDING WITH YOU WHEN ALL HELL BREAKS LOOSE. No matter what happens in the lives of the people I lead, I am there for them when they most need support.

I COMMIT TO A GOOD REPUTATION. Our actions matter—not just in the outcomes we deliver today, but in what people say about us, our organization, and our team tomorrow. I always make decisions that protect our good name.

So, if you are a leader and you say your organization loves its people, serves its people, supports its people, celebrates its people, is committed to its people, is all about its people, or any variation of these...but you *are not* yet living these ten specific commitments...then your words are out of alignment with your deeds. If you are serious about modeling the culture, you need to fix that, fast!

WHAT DOES LEADERSHIP BELIEVE ABOUT THE PEOPLE IN THE ORGANIZATION?

Leaders let the people in the organization know what we believe about them by the way they model the culture. For instance, we either believe our people are worth developing—worth investing time, energy, effort, attention, and financial resources in—or we do not. Our actions determine which it is. We can *say* whatever we want about our commitment to developing our people. But if there are no meaningful *examples* of it happening in real-time in a way that positively affects them, they are going to conclude that we do not believe in them or their potential or that our stated value of developing our people is not truly our value. And they will be right!

Never forget: A commitment is a positive standard that respects the rights of others and is *absolute*. The key word there, I believe, is *absolute*. When you make a relational commitment, you make it because you *love people and you truly care about people*, not because you think you will secure a short-term gain of some kind. A commitment means you are *all in, for good*. So, for instance, when you make a commitment to helping someone on your team develop to their fullest possible potential, you make that commitment knowing full well that the day may come when that person decides to move on and work somewhere else. In fact, you make and follow through on that commitment *hoping* that the person will grow and develop beyond the scope of the first job you designed for them.

When you are truly committed to someone's personal development, you continue to offer them, not just any opportunities, but the opportunities that are designed to help them grow—knowing full well that they may leave. And if they do leave, of course, you are not happy to see them go, but you are happy for what they are growing into. *This is modeling the culture.* You make and follow through on your commitment, *hoping* that they will turn into someone who charts their own path, someone who finds a newer and better way to make a difference. You trust that the relationship will pay dividends to *both of you* in the long term, and so you invest in that relationship with absolute commitment, knowing that if something is intended for you, it will present itself. In the meantime, you follow through on the commitment!

> "A good mentor hopes you move on. A great mentor knows you will."
> —Higgins, from the TV show *Ted Lasso*

Because accountable leaders are constantly modeling the commitment to grow their people, *their organization is growing.* Occasionally, someone might outgrow the organization, but these leaders know that if that happens, all that means is that they have done their job as a leader. This is the opposite of what many leaders model. Many leaders model *not* growing their people, and they constantly worry about who will leave next. Their priorities are upside down. They have forgotten that *growth itself* is what the best leaders aim to build the organization around! Sustainable organizational growth cannot happen if leaders do not make their own personal growth and the personal growth of others a cultural priority...and a non-negotiable commitment.

> Sustainable organizational growth cannot happen if leaders do not make their own personal growth and the personal growth of others a cultural priority...and a non-negotiable commitment.

In the next chapter, we will look at a particularly critical element of modeling the right culture: making sure you and the entire organization are modeling diversity, equity, and inclusion.

Chapter 10

Modeling Diversity, Equity, and Inclusion

THE MOST IMPORTANT asset a leader has in any organization is not money. It is not market share. The most important asset is the *trust of their people.*

With that trust, leaders can face and overcome challenges, achieve well beyond aggressive goals, and create highly creative and sustainable organizations. Without that trust, none of that is possible. The key cultural ingredient that makes trust possible can be summed up in a single, powerful word: *equity.* This is, at the end of the day, what leaders must model: a fundamental commitment to fairness, inclusion, and diversity. If leaders are not leading by example when it comes to equity, they are undercutting themselves and the organizations and teams who look to them for leadership.

> The key cultural ingredient that makes trust possible can be summed up in a single, powerful word: *equity.*

Modeling equity—or to use the most comprehensive phrase, diversity, equity, and inclusion—must be a priority, not just in the early going, but in the daily operation of the organization. Your values must incorporate equity, and your actions must support it in a prominent, direct, and impossible-to-ignore way. This is all about seeing people equally, valuing people equally, and seeking out and listening without judgment to differing perspectives that come from people who look different than we do and have different backgrounds and beliefs than we do. If we do not make a conscious effort to listen in this way, the working culture will suffer. And when the working culture suffers, potential suffers.

I am talking not just about listening that takes down facts. I am talking about the kind of listening that accepts the other person as our guide, the kind of listening that accepts that perspectives that differ from our own are important and life-giving, both on the individual level and the level of the organization. This kind of listening is rare, but I always see it in truly accountable leaders, and it always lies at the heart of organizations that manage to put into practice the core ideas of this book. This kind of listening challenges us to set aside what we think the answer is, open ourselves up to the insights and experiences of others, and unlock the deep and life-changing possibilities that come from true diversity of thought. This kind of listening demands being fully present in the moment. It demands that we proceed from the assumption that we always have something new and important to learn from every interaction and every shared instant of experience. This kind of listening, in short, is essential to the support of an organization that is not just diverse in terms of background and skin color, but diverse in terms of thought and outlook.

"Inclusivity means not just 'We're allowed to be there,' but 'We are valued.' Smart teams will do amazing things, but truly diverse teams will do impossible things."

—Claudia Brind-Woody

If you want a great culture, you have to tap into the richness of diversity. There has to be equity and inclusion. And your decision-making must model diversity, equity, and inclusion as strategic and operational priorities.

The tricky thing about this subject is that very often, we can imagine that we are modeling equity as leaders when in fact our actions are modeling something very different. What we say may be pointing in the right direction. But what do we *do* on a daily basis?

If we say that we are committed to diversity, equity, and inclusion, and we then surround ourselves with an executive team that looks like us, sounds like us, walks like us, talks like us, has the same kind of education we have, and goes out to lunch with us four out of five days of the week, then we are not modeling diversity, equity, and inclusion! All we are doing is digging ourselves into a deeper and deeper hole. The deeper that hole gets, the harder it is to sustain trust with the people who look to us for leadership.

When trust vanishes, engagement drops. And when engagement drops, communication suffers, innovation suffers, and the organization does not perform up to its potential. This is what happens when our values and our commitments do not support each other and do not align with and support diversity, equity, and inclusion. We get into the habit of engaging only with people who remind us of ourselves. Diversity is first and foremost about mental and experiential diversity, and these are significant organizational and competitive advantages. Why in the world would we choose to deprive ourselves of those advantages?

MOVE BEYOND THE EXCUSES

We work with a lot of executives who say things like:

Well, you know, we just don't have a lot of women apply-ing for these jobs. That's why the senior leadership team looks the way that it does. Women either don't have the right background or they don't want to work in this industry.

Or:

The people who end up moving into leadership roles in our organization tend to have XYZ qualifications. We're color-blind when it comes to assignments and promo-tions, but we do look for the right qualifications; and if the applicant doesn't have them, there's really not a lot we can do.

Or:

Honestly, I wish we did get more people of color applying for these jobs. There's just a lack of awareness, I think, about what the success profile looks like and how best to take advantage of the opportunities that exist. Beyond posting and advertising the openings and being clear about what the qualifications are, I really don't know what else we could be doing.

This is the sound of leadership *not* modeling diversity, equity, and inclusion! It is the sound of leadership making excuses.

There are countless things we could be doing. If we really believe that diversity, equity, and inclusion are important, then we will find a way to make it a priority. We will do more than just post an opening. We will seek people out. We will work our networks. We will make calls to colleges and universities. We will start discussions with government agencies and other entities tasked with getting marginalized communities into the workforce. We will create new conversations and new initiatives that will help us to identify the best and the brightest who happen to look a little different than we do. And we will keep doing that until we have gotten the best and the brightest onto the payroll, so that our team is open to talented people of any race, ethnicity, gender, age, or any other factor.

When it comes to modeling diversity, equity, and inclusion, the organization's senior leaders face a major question, a question that cannot be avoided if the leadership is serious about building up an Accountability Advantage: Are we looking for a way out, or are we looking for a way in?

> Are we looking for a way out,
> or are we looking for a way in?

If we are looking for a way *out*, we say things like, "I really wish there were more qualified women applicants and more qualified applicants of color for us to choose from." And we do nothing about it. Not only that, but we keep right on surrounding ourselves, during strategy sessions and social time, with people who look, talk, and think just like we do. Our actions tell the organization and the world that we just want the topic of diversity to go away. We want out of that conversation. That is not a commitment to IT'S ALL OF US!

On the other hand, if we are looking for a way *in*, we are constantly looking for, and finding, new ways to underwrite and support the fast-tracking of qualified people who will help us create a truly diverse organization, because we believe that is an important priority that is worth taking action on. And when lunchtime rolls around, we make sure that the people sitting around the table with us look, talk, and think like a cross-section of the world in which all of us live. And we listen. That listening is a critical part of the commitment to IT'S ALL OF US.

If we are serious about maximizing engagement and trust, we will be sure that we are looking for a way in, not a way out. And because we are looking for a way in, we will lead the way when it comes to both our professional interactions and our social interactions. Here as elsewhere in the modeling step, "Do as I say, not as I do" simply will not cut it as far as the senior leader is concerned!

IV

Teach the
CULTURE

Chapter 11

The Values Conversation

IT IS EASY, AT FIRST GLANCE, to confuse step two, Model the Culture, with step three, Teach the Culture.

Although there is some overlap and the two steps certainly do support each other, there are important distinctions between modeling and teaching, distinctions that everyone in the organization needs to understand. Let's examine those very briefly before we go any further.

Here is the difference:

> Modeling is all about the **senior leader** inspiring leaders (and others) in the organization to live the values and fulfill the relational commitments by means of the power of his or her personal example.
>
> Teaching is an ongoing conversation about what living the values and fulfilling the relational commitments actually looks like in practice—a conversation that involves **everyone** in the organization, that often uses true stories to reinforce cultural best practices, and that never ends.

The teaching step is multifaceted. It can start with formal training initiatives, but it will always extend far beyond those events. It is a consciously designed and deployed ongoing learning experience, and although it involves everyone, it always *begins* with the senior leader. This is the step where people begin to learn the depth of the values and how they are actually lived in this working environment. The power and inspiration of the senior leader's example is always there, thanks to step two, Model the Culture, and that example can serve as a kind of compass point for each individual member of each team. The leader is like a compass. True north is always true north. A compass is not complete unless it tells you where true north is. But even when you hold a compass in your hand, you still have to make the journey! The teaching step is where we make the journey—together.

> "Communication to a relationship is like oxygen is to life. Without it, it dies."
>
> —Tony A. Gaskins, Jr.

So, for instance, the teaching step may play out when someone starts a conversation about a specific issue, opportunity, challenge, or project that begs the question, *What does heading true north look like in this situation?* Other people start to contribute to that conversation, examples of best practices emerge, and the values become clear. That is teaching. And everyone is expected to do it, not just people in leadership positions.

Here are some more specific examples of what I am talking about:

Example 1. When we interview someone as a potential hire for our organization, we are obviously going to be looking for people who already have, or can easily align with, the values we embrace. Let's say one of those values is *Integrity*. The minute we talk about how, specifically, that value of *Integrity* would express itself in the daily activities and decisions of the job the person is applying for, that is teaching.

Example 2. When we hire and onboard that person, when we talk to them about what kinds of decisions do (and do not) look like *Integrity* on the job, when we share relevant stories that show what the value of *Integrity* looks like in action, and when the new team member gets clearer and clearer about what *Integrity* means *here,* at this organization, and how *Integrity* impacts their decision-making on a daily basis, that is teaching.

Example 3. Now say it is six months later, and everything we discussed with that team member has been internalized and put into practice on the job by that person. Now that same person we hired six months ago comes to us with an example of a place where they feel one of our organization's marketing initiatives is making misleading claims…and asks *us* for help in figuring out whether that marketing campaign aligns with *Integrity. We have an obligation to take part in that conversation with an open mind.* That is teaching, too! And if we reach a consensus during that conversation that there is an instance of misalignment with our stated value of *Integrity,* then we have an obligation to bring others in the organization into the conversation.

What I want you to notice is that this is always a *two-way* conversation about values. It is always a two-way conversation about the commitments we make to each other. It is never a lecture. The best teaching is never a monologue but rather a dialogue. And the best learning is always communal. Leaders have something to learn in these conversations. Followers have something to learn in these conversations. *We as an organization always have something to learn about how the values and the relational commitments will guide our next decisions and our next actions.* In other words, teaching never stops.

There are always teaching opportunities that show how to connect a decision and an action to our values and our relational commitments.

> We as an organization *always* have something to learn about how the values and the relational commitments will guide our next decisions and our next actions. In other words, teaching never stops.

Teaching must be built into everything we do, and that takes effort. We will know our organization is teaching consistently when *everyone* is talking spontaneously and in a heartfelt way about the organizational values and how those values apply to their world—without needing to be prompted to do so. So, for instance, if you are holding a team meeting that is scheduled to last 30 minutes, and at the end of that 30 minutes no one has mentioned the organizational values or how those values apply to the subjects being discussed and the decisions being made, then you are not yet teaching the values and the relational commitments consistently.

It is worth noting that one common mistake organizations make about teaching is imagining that no one with leadership responsibility has anything to learn about the culture. Jason Hansen, district manager at Wireless World, had this to say about that:

"We have weekly calls with all the store managers—it's a big group call—and one of the things I have to think about as the person tasked with leading that call is how to keep the core values alive. You know, there's a lot of energy right out of the gate when someone first learns about the values, and then if you're not careful, the discussion kind of loses its steam, just because the subject is not as new as it once was. And as the organization grows, of course, you get more and more people on the call who weren't in the room with you on the day the values were created. So as the person who's leading the call, I have to figure out how to keep the Wireless World values front of mind for people and also how to make sure that we are all still engaging with the values as part of a present-tense conversation, a conversation that connects to what we are all actually dealing with during the course of the day.

"One day, it occurred to me that, whenever you start a council meeting at church, you always open that meeting with a prayer. Why? Because that's who we are. That's what we're about. That's why we're there. Now obviously, this isn't church, but it seemed to me that structurally, you do want something like that at the top of a meeting, something that aligns everyone with who we are, what we're about, and why we're all here. And I thought, *Why don't we start every morning with a core value?*

"So that's what we have been doing. When you are a Wireless World store manager and you take part in that weekly call, you're going to hear about one of the core values at the very top of the call. You're going to hear exactly how we define that core value at Wireless World. And you're going to hear people sharing their own personal examples of what that value looks like in action."

This is a perfect example of a values conversation—and of making teaching an integral part of the culture.

Teaching is what empowers teams and individuals at all levels to step up, speak up, and put a stake in the ground whenever they notice someone making a choice that *does not* align with the organizational culture. Teaching is what illuminates and reinforces who we are, what we are about, and why we are here. Teaching is what lets people know that they have the right—and the duty—to call time-out whenever they notice someone (and by extension the entire organization) diverting from true north. And that is exactly what we want.

Chapter 12

The Power of Story

THE ACCOUNTABLE ORGANIZATION'S No. 1 tool when it comes to teaching is the *story*.

A memorable true story—long or short, recent or from the far distant past—can transform an entire organization and its culture. How? By making the core values and the relational commitments tangible and real for people. The effect of a great story that supports and clarifies the stated values is something close to magnetic. It engages people and enrolls them in the culture like nothing else. This is why we say that no effort to win the Accountability Advantage is complete without the action of sharing, repeatedly and with everyone in the organization, at least one true story that encapsulates and dramatizes one or more of the core company values.

> No effort to win the Accountability Advantage™ is complete without the action of sharing, repeatedly and with everyone in the organization, at least one true story that encapsulates and dramatizes one or more of the core company values.

As a practical matter, your organization will need a number of such true stories. But you will want to start by identifying *one* that you can share and share again. This must be a factual story that demonstrates instantly, to everyone who comes in contact with it, exactly who you are as an organization, exactly what you stand for, and exactly how you operate.

To illustrate the extraordinary power of starting with one powerful story, I want to take a moment to share with you the impact that a single extraordinary event can have when it is told and retold. The example I have in mind is a story that has had a huge impact for one of my clients, the Lubbock Economic Development Alliance (LEDA), a Texas nonprofit that has, for nearly two decades now, taken on the mission of "strengthening Lubbock's business community to ensure economic development and growth in our great city." I can tell you from personal experience that Lubbock *is* a great city and that LEDA gets great work done with some great people. It was my honor to work closely with LEDA to help them identify and put into words their unique, non-negotiable core values narrative, which appears below. I encourage you to study it closely because it is a model of a glove-fitting, and clearly articulated, values list.

LEDA: NON-NEGOTIABLE CORE VALUES

Attitude is Everything – A positive attitude projects internally and externally. A positive attitude is the key for encouraging, acknowledging and appreciating the work of others.

Be Trustworthy – Always do the right thing, even when no one is looking. Always respect each other, our community and our clients, remembering our word is our bond.

Communicate – Take a proactive approach to ensure that all levels of the team are informed in a professional and respectful manner. Express your ideas clearly when speaking and actively listen.

Family First – We expect you to perform at the same levels at home as you do at work. Excellence at home equals excellence at work.

Foster Success – Cultivate and encourage a forward-thinking environment that embraces creativity and diversity, providing support and resources that nurture each individual's unique skills. Empower and trust in others and strive for excellence. Be good stewards with our resources. All achievements big or small will be recognized.

Serve Others - Uncompromising commitment to our clients, our community and to each other.

Work in Wisdom – Work hard, work smart, produce while striving to achieve goals, and make good things happen. Be open and receptive to new ideas and guidance in your dealings with clients as well as fellow workers and be willing to share your experience and knowledge to produce and reach a successful result. Be a humble teacher; be a willing learner.

Let me emphasize that this is a *great* values narrative. It perfectly encapsulates what really matters to this organization and to the people who work for it. It says very clearly, *This is how we operate here.* But notice that like any list of values, it is still missing an essential complement—an example of how these values have actually played out in real life. For that, you need a *values story*, and one of the most powerful examples of this is a powerful story that I heard while working with LEDA.

A VALUES STORY FROM LEDA

True story: An employee at LEDA was diagnosed with a malignant tumor on her spine. To get treatment, she had to travel from Lubbock to the Mayo Clinic in Minnesota, and of course, the treatment meant she had to take a lot of time off from work. She quickly exhausted all of her available sick and personal days. She could not afford to be off work for all that time; she had a family to support. Without any encouragement from anyone in management, the other LEDA employees decided to do something about this situation. They went to the president and asked him to make a change in the organization's policy manual, a change that would permit them to *donate* their unused personal-time-off days to their colleague who had exhausted hers. The president agreed, and as a result, the employee's income stream kept flowing while she got treatment for her cancer.

How powerful is that?

There are a couple of important things to notice here. First and foremost, I want you to see how completely the employees at LEDA had *internalized* the following stated core values of the organization:

Be Trustworthy – (specifically:) Always do the right thing, even when no one is looking.

Serve Others – Uncompromising commitment to our clients, our community and to each other.

Foster Success – (specifically:) Cultivate and encourage a forward-thinking environment that embraces creativity and diversity.

These values, like the other values on their list, had attained such centrality in the lives of the LEDA employees that they had become second nature in their interactions and relationships *with each other*, both in and out of the workplace. If they had not been motivated by those values, they never would have made that request to the president! That is what happens when people come together around a set of values that inspires them and motivates them: *they become better human beings.* I cannot tell you the number of times I have had someone take me aside and tell me that as a result of working for one of the organizations that we have helped to create an Accountability Advantage, their spouse/partner/son/daughter/whatever has grown into a better, more generous, and more fulfilled person. That is how you know this is working!

The second thing I want you to notice is that this extraordinary story *defines* the organization through its values. It says, *This is who we are.* That is the power of a great story: it clarifies the values by bringing them to life in a dramatic situation, and it gives people a sense of identity, a sense of belonging, a sense of being part of something larger than themselves. Sharing a story like this *feels* good, because it spotlights exactly what the values look like in action, and it makes you feel more like a member of the team just for knowing that. When team members hear a story like this, they feel good about what they hear, and they want to pass it along to others. As a result of both the hearing and the telling, they find themselves better equipped to step up and take action that aligns with the values. Why? Because they have a better understanding of what the organization *is*, and as a result, they themselves are more closely connected with the organization. In sharing the story with others, they come to understand, at a deeper level, how the values should actually be lived.

> "The stories we live and tell provide coherence and meaning and orient our sense of purpose."
> —Sharon Daloz Parks

There is immense potential for personal transformation in a great list of values, but that potential can be leveraged only once people get a practical sense of *how* to tap into it. Hearing and sharing a story like this gives the members of the team that practical sense of *what the values look like in action*. It gives people a powerful example of "this is how we operate here," and it not only makes them want to share the story—it makes them want to create a new story of their own. So keep your eyes and ears open. Find a story like this that supports one or more of your organization's core values—a story you personally feel good about sharing with people.

As you consider which stories will best dramatize your values, which stories you and others will feel good about sharing, you will want to be on the lookout for events that capture:

- how your values show up in the ***decisions*** people make,
- how your values show up in the ***actions*** people take,
- and how your values show up in the ***impact*** those actions have on others.

All three of these must line up with the values. All three of these should show up in your story.

Also, you will want to make sure the stories you share illustrate not just what is happening on the outside, but what is happening on the inside of the organization. For example, if you choose to share a story about how you redesigned the organization's sales territories and you want to emphasize the values of *communication* and *collaboration,* the story you choose should not only illustrate how the territory redesign was communicated effectively to clients, but also how leadership communicated effectively with salespeople about what the new territory system should look like, how leadership made salespeople part of the decision-making process, and how relationships with both salespeople and clients improved under the new system.

And remember: If you do not see the values being lived internally, you can be sure you will not see them being lived in the external relationships with your clients, your customers, and your strategic allies!

> The values must be lived internally and must be evident in the way team members interact with each other before you can expect them to be lived consistently with clients, customers, and strategic allies.

A VALUES STORY FROM SOUTHWEST AIRLINES

I want to share an example of a powerful values story I came across that illustrates one of Southwest Airlines' core values, *Servant's Heart: Follow the Golden Rule, treat others with respect, and embrace our Southwest Family.* This story will stick with you forever:

Years ago, Herb Kelleher, the founder of Southwest, got word of a terrible tragedy: an employee's son had died in an automobile accident. The employee was in Baltimore; his family was in Dallas. Kelleher ordered a plane that was due to be taken out of service for maintenance to head to Baltimore so it could transport the employee to Dallas to be with his family right away. A Southwest employee later told a reporter: "Stories like that make me proud to work for this company." That story perfectly defines Southwest, and it clarifies exactly what a Servant's Heart is!

So, what is your organization's first values story? How does it illustrate the message "This is how we operate here"? Choose it carefully! Make sure the story you choose carries an emotional impact. The most powerful stories have a way of leaving the confines of the four walls of the organization. When stories connect with people emotionally, like the Southwest story I just shared with you, those stories get retold. They find their way into people's homes and spread throughout the community. This is how an organization becomes known for its culture, and it is one of the critical ways organizations attract, retain, and develop the most talented people.

A VALUES STORY FROM HAPPY STATE BANK

In an earlier chapter, I shared Happy State Bank's extraordinary (and judging by the bank's record of rapid growth and incredible profits, extraordinarily successful) list of values. You may recall that one of those values reads as follows: *Customer service is THE goal.* Those capital letters on the word "THE" begin to suggest how essential this value is…but there are a couple of true stories that Pat Hickman and company have been sharing for decades now that land the point even more powerfully. These two true accounts have shown Happy State's employees, and anyone else who is interested, just what the commitment to live that value looks like in action. Let me share both of them with you.

The first has to do with something we have all experienced: a declined payment. Once, when the bank was making updates to their computer system, there were a few problems with some customers' debit cards. A customer who had been grocery shopping at Walmart called the bank and told them that her card wasn't working. Most banks that compete with Happy State would have apologized for the problem, explained that the system was being worked on, thanked the customer for her patience, and assured her that the problem would be resolved just as soon as possible. But since *Customer service is THE goal* at Happy State Bank, and since that value is explicitly connected in the mission statement with the Golden Rule of doing unto others as we would have them do unto us, the teller who took that call *did not* choose the well-traveled road most organizations would have gone down. That teller knew that leaving that customer stranded at the checkout line was not in keeping with either the mission or the values. She knew that customer had just spent an hour filling her shopping cart with the groceries her family needed for the week. And she knew from her own personal experience how time-consuming and aggravating it was to do all of that, swipe the card, and be told that the purchase had not gone through. So while she was still on the line with the customer, the teller found out how much the amount due was—and she debited the customer's account for that amount. Then she asked the customer where she was, took the money out of the cash drawer, and drove to Walmart to meet the customer in person—and pay for those groceries in cash!

The point here is twofold. First, the teller lived the stated values. Second, Hickman and the other leaders at Happy State Bank made a point of *sharing* this true story with everyone in the organization so that people would know exactly what living the values looks like!

ANOTHER VALUES STORY FROM HAPPY STATE BANK

Here is another powerful true story from Happy State Bank that has been shared internally for years. It has to do with the way Happy State Bank handles "operating hours." Although the lobby of each Happy State branch technically "opens" at 9 A.M. and "closes" at 4 P.M.—because those are the posted hours of operation—in practice, the bank operates differently. In practice, the doors are unlocked 15 minutes early and they stay unlocked, and the employees stay there to serve you for another half hour beyond the official closing time! Employees are celebrated and acknowledged whenever they take care of a customer's issue "after hours." There have been hundreds of such stories over the years.

When I asked Pat why he did business that way, he asked, "Have you ever tried to get to the bank by 4 P.M., and gotten there at 4:05 P.M., and found the doors locked and the place empty?"

I said, "Sure."

He said, "How did that make you feel?"

I said, "Lousy—even though I knew it was my fault I was late."

He said, "We don't want people to feel that way."

What I want you to notice here is that for Pat, for his executive team, and for every individual employee who has been empowered to live this value with customers, *the focus is on how people feel*, not on the rules that must be followed.

This is a critical distinction. If *Customer service is THE goal*, that means we are thinking less about the rulebook and more about how our actions make other people *feel*. That is Pat's way of thinking as a person, and it is the *organizational* way of thinking in place at Happy

State Bank. And you know what? The minute Pat shared the true story of Happy State Bank's operating hours with me, it became my way of thinking, too! That story was so powerful and had such a remarkable, immediate impact on me that I now make it my goal to use that same filter in *all* of my interactions with people. As a result, I am constantly asking myself the question, *How do I want to make people feel because of this conversation?*

From where I sit, this story made living the Golden Rule contagious! The fact that I "caught" it in that moment illustrates the immense power of, first, committing to and living your value and, second, discovering and sharing powerful stories about what those values look like in action. When you do that—when you impact and evolve someone's way of thinking like this experience evolved mine—you help the person who comes in contact with that story, whether they work for you or not, to become a better person. That is the value and impact of a great values story.

For Pat and for Happy State Bank, the Golden Rule is non-negotiable. It is easy to *say* that, of course. But these two true stories from Happy State Bank show people what that really looks like in action.

What is *your* organization's first values story?

Chapter 13

"The Entire Team Bought In"

JOHN OSBORNE is the CEO of LEDA, the Texas nonprofit I mentioned a little earlier. Recently, I had a discussion with John about the impact that teaching the values has had on his team. Here is some of what he had to share.

How long has it been now since we worked together on defining, modeling, and teaching your values?

It's been six years since we worked with you, and in that time I've become a huge advocate for you and your processes. They have been transformational for us as an organization. I've taken our work on accountability out to many of my peers, and some great people have come to work for us as a result of our culture that we have here. The fun part about all this is that in reality, you didn't change our culture; you have helped us to formalize it and have it be where the entire team bought in. It was a moment of enlightenment almost, one that touched everybody. That's what defining, modeling, and teaching the values has done for us. Everybody bought in.

How have your hiring practices changed?

When we have people that want to come to work for us, a really interesting conversation plays out now, one that didn't play out before we worked with you. We now say, basically, "This is it. This is who we are, and it's okay if your core values are different. But this is us. If these are not your core values, it's quite alright; all that means is that this isn't the place for you to come to work." So that's certainly a very early teaching moment, maybe one of the most important ones, and moments like that, with new people and people who have been with us for a while, have had a huge impact.

What kind of impact? How would you say the work we did together changed what you and your organization have been able to achieve?

I would say since we worked with you our activity has tripled—with a leaner staff. For example, we used to have a seven-person marketing team. We now have a five-person marketing team that is significantly more effective and productive than before. That's largely a result of some people who didn't buy into the values moving on to other opportunities and the people who stayed being empowered by that. Sometimes when someone moves on, that is protecting the culture, of course, but it was also a teaching moment for everyone, because that really clarified the values. And as a result, there have been some major leaps forward in our activity and our achievements as an organization, and we're quite proud of that.

Why has your team become more productive, in your opinion?

When you have a high-functioning team that all has the same kind of core values, what you find is that people strive for greatness. And that striving for greatness is not just something they do for themselves. It is them as an organization. It's us as a team, as an organization. And because of what our core values are, we put that team-first, community-first, client-first mindset out as a way of living and working. People encounter that, and they see it as striving for greatness and they want to be a part of it. They want to do something big. It has really been transformational. A rising tide floats all boats! I want to say something important, though: A big part of teaching is simply identifying where the values match up and then empowering people. Someone either has the value or they don't. I can't really teach someone to be trustworthy. They either are or they aren't. But what you can teach them is that by living the value consistently, as part of the team, they can be something bigger than themselves. And you can share all the examples of the times when people do live the values. And that is exciting. That inspires people.

TEACHING THE VALUES TO PEOPLE WHO HAVE NEVER EVEN HEARD OF THEM

I spoke at length with Jason Hansen, district manager at Wireless World. Our subject was an important one: how the teaching step plays out when you must integrate people and teams into your organization—people who do not yet share or perhaps even know anything about the values you have defined. Here are some of the highlights of that conversation:

What does teaching the Wireless World culture look like in your world lately?

We recently acquired a company with 10 stores, which meant we had to find a way to share, explain, and reinforce the Wireless World values with all the new people who were coming on. There were about 30. To do that, we had to take into account where these people were already, meaning we had to get a sense of the working culture that was in place before we got there and respond to that. We wanted to meet them where they were.

I ended up being one of the people tasked with leading that effort. This was totally unexpected. This came at me with zero time to prepare, because I learned about the acquisition on a webinar and right away I was given this assignment, which meant I had to get up to speed very quickly. So I did some digging, I talked to some people at the company whose stores we had just acquired, and I tried to figure out what kind of culture we had just inherited.

So what did you learn?

One of the things I learned about this company was that a lot of the values discussion had been dominated by the goal of delivering great customer service. There's nothing wrong with serving the customer, of course; that's extremely important. But in terms of the values, it just wasn't a very holistic approach. The only value people could talk about was "make sure the customer is satisfied," which is not enough.

And so, as we started working more closely with the people in those stores, what really jumped out at me was that they had been operating without much of a compass. I don't know that I saw a clear mission statement or core values in the leadership style that people had been working under. It was very top-down: "You work for me. I tell you what to do. I am your boss. Never forget that customer service is our No. 1 priority." That was about it. So these people who were now working as members of the Wireless World team had a pretty limited sense of autonomy when it came to doing their job. Basically, they were controlled by their immediate superior, which is not how we operate. They didn't come to work and think, *What should we do to be better?*

Or: *How can we deliver a great experience for the customer?* They came to work and waited for instructions, which is definitely not the Wireless World culture.

That sounds like a classic example of a culture by default.

Yes.

So what did you do? Have you been able to shift that thinking?

Two and a half months in, we are definitely moving the needle. One reason for the shift has been a best practice we do in all of our stores, which is to be sure to talk about the values, explicitly and in detail, at every daily team meeting. We really focus on the core values. It was a quick transition, so we ran into a couple of potholes along the way when it came to making that a reality at these stores, but we did find a way to make that part of the daily routine.

What kinds of potholes?

Very early on, we had distributed some posters to reinforce the values. Only trouble was, they had an abbreviated version of the values. In putting together that poster, the print shop had done their own little edit pass on the way the Wireless World values were phrased, and of course, we had spent a lot of time with you, Sam, getting them just right. We wanted the collateral that people saw during the working day and during meetings to match the actual values we had defined. We phrased them the way we phrased them for a reason. And when we saw the changes, we just laughed.

What kinds of changes had they made?

Instead of "Be accountable," they had listed the value as "Accountability." Well, that's like watering down the product. It's not accountability, the concept. It's us making a commitment to each other to *be* accountable. We called the value "Be accountable" for a reason, because that's the value we actually live, day in and day out, and so that's the value we talk about: "Be accountable." And similarly, they had changed "Serve the community" to "Community service." I guess they thought "Community service" sounded better, but the challenge is, that is not the value. We are not talking about some abstract expression of the idea of serving the community. We are talking, again, about a personal commitment: *We serve the community.* These were the kinds of changes that might have seemed like a little thing to someone coming in contact with the values for the very first time, but to us it was a very serious problem. Those weren't the Wireless World values. People had to be looking at the right values. So we went to a print shop and had all the posters done all over again with all the correct verbiage, including the definitions of each value. We believe the definitions matter because these are our definitions—you can't google these.

So what was the most important resource you used in teaching the values to this group?

No doubt about it—it was the values narrative. We came back to that again and again. I made people read the core values and the narrative that describes each value out loud at the start of every day. The definitions are critical. Definitions matter. We wanted people to see those definitions on the walls of every store, and we wanted people to hear them and speak them every day. At every meeting, my message was basically, "Okay, this is what we believe. When you show up at work, I expect this from you. And I'm telling you, you need to understand not just the first few words of the value but the entire definition because you can't google this stuff. If you want to know what *Be accountable* actually means for you on a daily basis, this piece of paper right here tells you what it means to us. Not something you find online." It's much, much more important that they understand who we are than that they cross something tactical off the to-do list, so I focus very heavily on the values narrative in the early going. And that is what has moved the needle. You start seeing little wins, and then you reinforce those wins. You see little examples where they are doing behaviors that match up with the values, and you call that out at the team meetings, and the group kind of goes, "Got it."

Anything else you feel would be important to share with someone who finds themselves tasked with doing a similar job—teaching the values?

I would just add this: If it's the right set of values—by which I mean a set of values that people can benefit from living both at home and at work—then I would keep an ear out for the "aha moment" that often happens when people realize that for themselves, because that is someone who will help you to spread the message. That has happened to me multiple times. That's the point where you know for certain that people really do get it. I've had managers come up to me and say, "Jason, what I realized is if I follow these core values, I'm going to have a good life. It's not just about here at the store. If I take this home and make this part of my interactions with family and with everyone else, I will live a good life." Now, when I hear that, I know I have an ally when it comes to teaching the values, because that is exactly how it is for me. I was talking to my wife last night, and I said, "Hey, I'm going to meet with Sam and talk about the core values. Would you agree we use the Wireless World core values at home with our daughters?" We have three daughters: seven, ten, and twelve. And without missing a beat, she says, "You mean *attitude of gratitude*?" I said, "Yeah." "You mean *admit your mistakes and fix them fast*?" I said, "Yeah." We went down the whole list. They were all there. My wife and I had built our whole parenting approach around the Wireless World values. That's a good sign, I think. It's a validation that you've defined the right values in the first place because they're something you can use to become a better parent and a better person.

THE BIG TAKEAWAYS ON TEACHING THE CULTURE

Here are some major takeaways we make a point of sharing with clients about Teaching the Culture.

At the end of day, all any leader has is impact and influence. The leader's personal commitment to live and teach a great set of values is the only thing that can be relied upon, in the long term, to maximize that leader's opportunity for positive impact and positive influence.

The leader teaching the values and fulfilling the commitments is what brings out the greatness in people, and bringing out that greatness is the essence of the leader's job description. People see the leader's level of personal commitment and want to commit to that level of commitment themselves. This is, in a cultural sense, the only teaching moment that really matters.

When people receive that kind of teaching from the leader, it means they, too, want to be committed to living and teaching those same values, not just in the organization but in their personal lives. This is how you can tell whether you are teaching values that connect to a carefully designed, consistently modeled organizational culture: your teaching impacts not just team members, customers, and stakeholders, but the family members of all those people and the community in which those people live. When you are doing this right, you are bringing out the very best in your organization's people, in all realms of their life. One of the most satisfying parts of my job is hearing friends and family members tell me, "Since you started working with our organization, (name) has become a better spouse/parent/friend/you name it." And I can tell you that I have been blessed to hear that often. It makes me grateful for my own calling as a teacher.

However, that inspiring outcome happens only when the person teaching the values and the commitments *personally believes them to be important in their own life* and is willing to live by them. That means the organization's first teacher, the senior leader, has to begin the teaching by setting the example in words and actions in all areas of their own life. If that is not taking place, the teaching step is not only not fulfilled—it hasn't even begun. Teaching *requires* engagement from the organization as a whole, but it always *begins* with the leader's personal commitment. If that is missing, nothing happens.

In addition to maintaining a high level of personal commitment to the values and the relational commitments, I would share these four go-to strategies for those eager to make sure the teaching step takes root.

Go-to strategy #1: Share the value narratives frequently. Repeating only the first word or two of the values does not make the richness of the value clear, and it does not inspire people to live the values. The narrative answers the question, *What does it mean to live this value at the highest level?* That is what you are teaching. A poster will not do it. A bumper sticker will not do it. Constantly returning to the narratives, discussing them, and asking people what that value would look like in their life if they implemented the narrative *does* do it. People need to hear and speak the value narratives.

> People need to hear and speak the value narratives.

Go-to strategy #2: Talk about the values often. Remember: If a meeting has concluded and you have not mentioned one or more of the values, you have not led the meeting properly! We tell our clients: "Once you start talking about the values, you can never stop." The subject of how to live the values is never exhausted. When you stop talking about your values and how your decisions connect to them, your people begin to see the values as unimportant. If your values are really important, you will never end the values conversation.

Go-to strategy #3: Rotate the values discussions. Do not fixate on one value. Focus on them all. Bear in mind that the power of values lies in teaching and living a great *set* of values.

Go-to strategy #4. Mention the culture frequently, not just the individual values that define it. Look for ways to work the words "our culture" into your conversations as often as possible. Talk about what "our culture" makes possible, what examples of "our culture" look like in action, and how "our culture" enables us to change people's lives for the better. Talk about the benefits of being a part of "our culture." Teaching the culture means talking about the culture. The more often people talk about the culture, the easier it will be for them to live it!

> Teaching the culture means talking about the culture. The more often people talk about the culture, the easier it will be for them to live it!

V

Protect the CULTURE

Chapter 14

No Weak Link

YOUR ORGANIZATIONAL CULTURE is only as strong as its weakest link. But your culture does not have to have a weakest link.

> All the work you and your team have done up to this point can be undone by a *single* person who refuses to live the values or fulfill the relational commitments.

All the work you and your team have done up to this point can be undone by a *single* person who refuses to live the values or fulfill the relational commitments. This is because culture by default requires zero maintenance and spreads like wildfire, while a culture by design requires constant maintenance, reinforcement, and protection and must be carefully cultivated via a personal commitment to *every* relationship. The fourth step of our process, Protecting the Culture, is all about making sure that the progress you have made up to this point does not vanish because one person feels like drilling a hole in the boat. It is about making sure that everyone on the boat truly wants to be on the boat and wants to make the voyage a success.

Protecting the culture is what happens when we take conscious, thoughtful action to preserve, maintain, and defend the values that have been defined, modeled, and taught. Although anyone in the organization can protect the culture, leadership has the primary duty to fulfill this step. In fact, this is the core of the leader's job description. Protecting the culture is a far more important priority for the leader, and especially for the senior leader, than any tactical responsibility (such as securing a big deal).

When leadership takes on that priority as a personal commitment, truly amazing things are possible. I have already told you about the remarkable success story that is Happy State Bank. This next story illustrates just how seriously they take the protecting step.

Once, I was delivering a presentation to a group of business leaders in Texas. Here is what I said to the group: "We've all had the experience of being in the presence of someone who has a negative attitude. Of course we don't enjoy that experience. It brings us down, and it brings the entire organization down. I'm curious: How many of you work with someone who has a negative attitude? If you do, just raise your hand."

All the hands in the room went up—except for one man. Both of his hands stayed down.

The gentleman who did not raise his hand was Mikael Williamson, who was at that time president of Happy State Bank.

I asked him: "You didn't raise your hand. Was that on purpose?"

He said, "Yes."

I said, "Why didn't you raise your hand?"

His answer stunned the group. "At Happy State Bank," he said, "people with a negative attitude aren't allowed to stay on. If they have a negative attitude, we help them find another place to work. We don't let them keep working at our bank."

What we all heard when he said those words was the sound of leadership in action.

That leader's commitment is to *live the values*. One of the values at Happy State Bank is *Attitude is everything*. Now, the leader either lives the values or does not live the values. The leader either allows the negative attitude to happen…or doesn't. At Happy State Bank, leaders do not allow it to happen! Starting at the top!

Consider what you could accomplish in your organization if *your* senior leadership took the same approach. Imagine an organization where people with a negative attitude were simply not allowed to stay on, once they demonstrated clearly that the habit of living the negative attitude was more important to them than the habit of living the values. Think about what you could do if you protected the culture without apology or hesitation *every time* there was a breakdown. Think about what would be possible if someone who did not buy into your core values got all the coaching, all the support, all the encouragement they could possibly expect so they could learn what it means to buy into the values…and then, if that person ended up not being willing or able to do that, think about how the experience of working for your organization would change if they got to move on and work somewhere else.

Think about it: What would your organization be capable of if there *were* no cultural weak link? If only people who chose to align with the values were allowed to stay on? If everyone on your team bought into the values, lived the values, and showed up for work each day because that's really what they wanted to do?

What would your world be like if the people everyone knows would really rather be working somewhere else *actually worked somewhere else?*

These are the empowering questions you will be exploring in this part of the Accountability Advantage™. Answering them in an account-able way requires a level of courage that not every leader possesses. But developing and exercising that courage yields a prize whose value is hard to calculate: *a high-performance working culture people want to be part of.*

> "Courage is the main quality of leadership, in my opin-ion, no matter where leadership is exercised. Usually it implies some risk, especially in new undertakings."
> —Walt Disney

If you are serious about making that kind of culture a daily reality in your organization, you will implement step four. The chapters in this section show you how to do that.

Chapter 15

Protecting the Culture... with People Who Have Never Lived the Culture

THAT STORY ABOUT Mikael Williamson choosing not to raise his hand is one of my personal favorites, and I share it often. During a recent interview, founder Pat Hickman gave me more important insights to share when he started talking about how serious he has always taken the job of protecting the culture at Happy State Bank. One particularly critical challenge arises when an organization that has already done the work to define, model, and teach a high-performance working culture acquires another organization that has not.

"As soon as we announced that we were buying another bank," Pat said, "I always made it a point to visit every office of that bank in person. For instance, when we bought Centennial Bank, I went to every branch. That's 17 offices spread all over the state of Texas. The first wave of meetings after the Centennial acquisition was probably the most challenging part of that particular schedule. I remember I went to over a dozen meetings in a two-day period of time. But I made it a priority to conduct all those meetings in person, because protecting the culture is a critical conversation, and it has to be conducted in a way that gets that fact across. So when I walked in to meet each branch manager at what used to be Centennial so I could have that conversation in person, here's what I would say:

> "You have no reason to trust me, because I'm getting ready to turn your world upside down. You are now part of Happy State Bank. And I'll tell you something important: what we do at Happy State Bank we like, and what we do works. If you will embrace our culture, you are going to do just fine. So here are our values, right here on these sheets. Read them, understand them, live them, and you're going to fit with us just like a charm. If not, it's going to be ugly. That is the truth.

> "So first off, let's just talk about a couple of items. If you're somebody who likes to whine, if you're somebody who just likes to complain all the time, I'm going to tell you right now, you really need to go polish off your resume and start looking for another job, rather than waiting until we let you go, because you're not going to fit with us at all. You will go. In fact, if that's your M.O., I've heard that they're hiring down at the DMV. You could go talk to those people; you'd probably fit in great down there. If you're not going to make it here, you need to get ready for that.

> "Now, starting today, we're going to be asking you to do some really dumb stuff. We know that some of the stuff that we do is not as good as some of the stuff you do. We want you to do it anyway. At this bank, you have a little over 100 employees. We have over 800 employees.

Now, in the middle of a conversion, in the middle of an acquisition like this, it's like a battlefield. There's no time to change ammunition and strategy in the middle of the war. You don't have time to change how you're fighting the war. And it's going to be a lot easier to change 100 people than it is going to be to change 800 people. So here's what I want you to do: Do the stuff we ask you to do, even though it is stupid. Don't whine when we ask you to do stupid stuff. Accept ahead of time that we will be asking you to do stupid stuff—and do it. Every time we ask you to do something that you know for a fact is stupid, I want you to write it down. Here's a special notepad I want you to use for that. You'll see that printed across the top of each sheet is the headline STUPID STUFF HAPPY DOES. I want you to use this pad to write down what all that stupid stuff is. Every time you find yourself being asked to do something stupid, jot down the details here. Do that, and I promise you we will be back one year from now, and we will say to you, 'Talk to us about all the dumb stuff we made you do.' And you know what? Every time you help us to find stuff that we need to fix, we will fix it. But right now, we don't have time to fix it. We need to wait until we're out of the battle to talk about the stupid stuff. Later on, we can go in and we can fix those things.

"That was what I said, over and over again, to each branch manager, and it always worked. But the only reason it worked is that they believed we would keep our word, and we always did. A year later, we would always go in and review their list of stupid stuff that they felt needed to be changed, and we would hear them out; and if something needed fixing, we would fix it.

"So if you are willing to keep your promises, which of course you need to be, this strategy is very effective. In fact, people love it. I highly recommend this approach to anybody who has taken over another company and wants to protect the culture."

We work with many organizations that embark on merger and acquisitions projects, some of them quite substantial (as Happy State Bank's have been over the years). Leadership's goal in these situations is simple: they want the teams and organizations they are taking on to live by the same high-performance culture that allowed them to thrive, grow, and succeed *before* they were in a position to launch a merger and acquisitions project! The key to making this happen should be obvious by now: *mastering and protecting the core values in their own world first.* You cannot protect the values in a new team or organization if you are not protecting them in your own organization! By the way, "protecting and defending the culture" is always the first line item in Happy State Bank's annual strategic plan. That is as it should be for *every* organization that aspires to a high-performance working culture.

> Make "protecting and defending the culture" the first line item in your annual strategic plan.

DEFENDING YOUR ORGANIZATION FROM "CULTURAL DRIFT"

Listen to what Ron Mittelstaedt, CEO of Waste Connections, has to say on the same topic of protecting the culture with people who have not yet lived it:

When you look at a potential acquisition, how does organizational culture impact your decision about whether to make that acquisition?

Well, you know, it is absolutely something we look at. We're buying generally smaller, privately owned, first-, second-, third-generation family-owned-and-controlled companies. Many of those are what I call "hierarchy-driven management cultures." Their style is basically top-down. The attitude is pretty much "do as I say, not as I do"—sort of a 1950s command-and-control style leadership and ownership. While that way of running a company can work well in the accomplishment of objectives, it's not something most employees today are thrilled with, and it's not part of our culture. So when we look at that, we often tell people flat-out that they are going to be a lot happier in a new organization than in the current company, because that is just not how we operate.

Is that a difficult discussion?

In practice, it is actually relatively easy to address this. You have skeptics who think, *Well, you can't really run a company that way.* And we sit them down and tell them, "You know what, servant leadership really is what we are all about, and the role of the leader is to be accountable to employees, because that's what makes employees accountable to the leader. So accountability really is what we are all about. And being involved in the community is what we are about. And so is empowering our employees to make day-to-day decisions." That is a big shift for some people. At Waste Connections, employees really are empowered to do anything they feel is appropriate within a very tight boundary. Anything outside of that boundary has to go up to someone else who can make that decision, but inside that boundary, they have autonomy. So we tell the skeptics, "This really is how we operate, and if all of that is not a good fit for you, then we would certainly understand if you felt you needed to go find someplace else to make a contribution. You would not be the first to reach that conclusion. But this is how we run our business."

Can you talk a little bit more about empowering team members? Because I know that is a really essential element of your culture.

We believe that if you give people the tools and the resources and the knowledge, they'll make the right decision 99 percent of the time. And they'll make those decisions on the spot, which allows you as leaders not to have to make thousands of micro-decisions a day that you're already paying someone to do. Let them make the decision. We find that most people find that refreshing and respond positively to it, even though it takes some adjustment. And again, if they ultimately decide they don't like our values and they don't agree with them and they can't embrace them, they're probably not going to be around long.

So what are the challenges you face when you do bring in an organization and you know for certain that their culture isn't your culture?

The major challenge, in that case, is staying consistent with what you say you're about.

You have to know what's important, and you have to defend that because it can get tough. Let's say you've just taken on an organization, and their actions and decisions tell you right away that they don't really believe safety is that important. They believe safety is a cost of doing business. Well, we believe that safety guides every decision, period. We believe we have no alternative to making safety a priority. For us, it's not a cost of doing business; it's *how* we do business. We believe that while you may never get to a world where there are no incidents, that's still the objective. It's just a very different approach, and so you have to draw the line. So when you buy a large organization and you've got a lot of people who don't agree with that way of looking at safety and who want to push back on that, you have to be careful. If you ever find yourself saying, "Well, let's let them do it their way for six months and see what happens," that is not where you want to be. That is a losing proposition. That's when you let the values start sliding. You just can't do that.

> "If you ever find yourself saying, 'Well, let's let them do it their way for six months and see what happens,' that is not where you want to be. That is a losing proposition. That's when you let the values start sliding. You just can't do that."
> —Ron Mittelstaedt, CEO, Waste Connections

We sometimes call that "cultural drift."

Right. So that's really dangerous. The toughest thing is building up the personal and organizational courage necessary to be sure you are sticking to those values from day one and recognizing that things are going to get rocky along the way, but even if they get rocky, you need to stay the course and, if necessary, invite people to go work somewhere else. Because if you compromise on the values, that's when you cause the boat to really go side to side.

So you're saying that leaders need to be comfortable with a certain level of discomfort?

Exactly. Sticking with the values can sometimes feel uncomfortable for leaders. In the short term, it can feel uncomfortable for employees and uncomfortable for customers. But you have to stay at it. And yes, people will have the choice of either leaving or changing their behavior. But in our experience, it's best for them to reach that decision point quickly. You don't want this kind of thing to drag out over time. You want to rip the Band-Aid off and say, "Okay, that's done. Let's go. Let's move on." If the values really mean something, that is what you have to do. If they are real, they are real whether or not they are convenient or popular. If they are real, they are real whether or not it is easy to live them or tough to live them. It's all very well to talk about the values when they are what people want to hear. That's easy. It's talking about them and living them when it's not what somebody wants to hear that is most important."

Now that you've heard firsthand from two leaders with a proven track record of protecting the culture, it's time to look at how you can complete this step in your own world.

Chapter 16

The Four Words You Need to Know When It Comes to Protecting the Culture

IF SOMEONE TOLD ME I had only four words to share on the topic of protecting the culture—four words and only four words that I could ask each leader in the organization to jot down on a sticky note and then post in a spot where they would definitely be seen each and every day—then the words I would choose would be these:

Hire slow, fire fast.

> Hire slow, fire fast.

Take your time on hires, and make sure the person you are considering has a value set that aligns perfectly with yours. Clean house quickly when you get clear evidence that somebody on your team cannot or will not live the values, because whatever advantage you think you are enjoying by keeping this person in the organization does not justify sabotaging your culture.

Hire slow, fire fast sounds simple, and it is simple…but it is not easy. It takes work, discipline, and courage to implement, particularly in the early going. But the investment always pays off.

This one powerful standard, I believe, lies at the heart of the protecting step. It is the engine that has driven the success experienced by all the organizations I interviewed for this book. If you are not currently hiring slow and firing fast—and most of the organizations I run into are doing exactly the opposite—then you need to change course. If you are serious about building a high-performance culture, you will hire slow and fire fast.

"YOU'VE GOT A DUTY TO PROTECT YOUR PEOPLE"

The *Hire slow, fire fast* principle is the engine of the astonishing long-term growth and profitability trajectory of Happy State Bank, encompassing not one but two major recessions. The bank, you may recall, began with a single location in a small Texas town most people had never heard of, but the bank currently boasts 61 locations and almost $7 billion in assets. As I interviewed Happy State Bank chairman Pat Hickman for this book, I found that he had some important things to say on the subjects of hiring and firing. In fact, he may be the wisest voice I have ever heard on these critical topics. So I invite you to listen closely to him now on the non-negotiability of this way of thinking about work, leadership, and growing the business.

What is your philosophy when it comes to personnel decisions?

I believe you've got a duty to protect your people, a duty to protect the culture, with every hiring and firing and retention decision you make. So you have to be certain you don't compromise your principles. Ever. There is just no valid reason to keep someone on the team who does not live your values—not one. You look for the cream of the crop, the people who rise to the top and *also* buy into your values and agree to live them. You hold on to those people. You let the superstars shine. And you say goodbye, quick, to the people who don't want to live the values. They will flash on your radar screen at some point. It doesn't take long. The minute you see that flash, you say, "Let's let that person go." That's my philosophy when it comes to personnel decisions.

Have you ever felt bad about letting someone go who doesn't want to live the values?

Sam, you know my feeling about Providence. My attitude is that God controls. I don't believe that a leaf falls off of a tree that God doesn't make fall. I don't believe that a hair can come out of your head but God plucked it. God knows everything about us. Also, I believe that all things work together for good. If they don't fit in here, God's got a better plan for them to be somewhere else. Let me tell you, I worked in a company back in the mid '80s, for a bank in the mid '80s in Texas, when we saw thousands of banks fail. My company that I was working for at that time had 800 employees, and over an 18-month period we cut it back to 250. We had to lay off 550 people. Do you know, I tracked a bunch of those folks down and talked to them about what happened, and every single one of them but one, if you tracked them down today and asked them about what happened back in the 1980s, will look you in the eye and tell you that being laid off was the best thing that ever happened to them. They say things like, "This allowed me to take stock and go off and pursue a different career, a career that was better for me." Or: "Being laid off allowed me to get closer to my wife and my kids. It was the right thing for me at the time." Out of all the people I talked to, there was one who was bitter about it, one woman who never let it go. I think she went to her grave bitter. I believe she had a miserable life. All that reminds me of is *attitude is everything.* Attitude, attitude, attitude.

When you make a decision like this, and you're a leader, here's what you're thinking: *I've also got to take care of everyone who is working hard and living the values.* At the end of the day, it's about being fair, all the way around the board.

I run into a lot of leaders who say they can't let someone go because it's going to be difficult to fill the slot with someone new. What's your advice to—

No, no, no, if it's a rotten apple, get it out of there, because it's going to spoil the whole bunch. There have been times that I've let somebody go because they weren't fitting in, and it took us months to fill that slot. So what? You don't compromise principles. You don't settle for second best, because if you do, you're going to find yourself in this same mess all over again—and maybe worse. Wait until you get the right one. What I have found is that the wait is always worth it to get the right folks on board.

> "You don't settle for second best, because if you do, you're going to find yourself in this same mess all over again—and maybe worse."
> —Pat Hickman, founder, Happy State Bank

THE CRAPPY DAY

If you work at Happy State Bank, you are allowed to have 364 happy days over the course of a year…and you are allowed to have one crappy day. What a stroke of genius! Why wouldn't every organization on earth adopt this policy? We would all have fewer people experiencing crappy days at work to deal with.

"If you decide you need to take that crappy day for yourself," Pat Hickman explains, "that's fine. Just do it at home, and yes, you can do it with pay. If that's the kind of day you're having, get the heck out of here. We don't want you to rub off on everybody else. Go home and do whatever you need to do for that day. Bring misery to your own house, but don't leave it here. Now, every once in a while, we have a situation where people have already taken their crappy day, and then, six months later, they're treating one of their coworkers lousy. You know what we do? We sit them down in private, and we say, 'Hey, you know what? I checked your records, and you already had your crappy day this year. You've got to go fix this. We don't have time for this. This isn't the place for you to act the way you're acting. Go work it out with Sue, and fix your attitude.' And they do!"

This may be the most creative technique yet for protecting the culture! And it reinforces the *Hire slow, fire fast* principle. Someone you take your time finding—someone who already lives the values— really should not need more than one crappy day a year!

Chapter 17

Front End, Back End

MOST OF THE TIME, leaders we work with are interested in protecting the culture by responding to specific *events*—for instance, having a conversation with someone when they see that person violating the values by disrespecting a fellow team member, or letting someone go when they prove to you, by repeated behavior, that they are not living the values and not interested in living the values. These actions are important…but they do not give us the full picture. Responding to these events in the moment is what we call protecting the culture on the *back end*. We are responding to specific actions, ones that are not acceptable within our culture. But what about what happens to protect the culture on the front end?

What about the relationships, the discussions, and the mutual support that can *change* people's habits over time…help them to align with the values…and make them better human beings? What about the conversations that will make it easier for them to make changes in their thinking and behavior in the future, changes that support the values? To make that kind of change happen, we need meaningful person-to-person discussions on the *front end*.

Here is an example that will help to illustrate what I mean.

Let's assume you and I work together. Let's also assume that one of the values our organization has taken on, and that you and I have agreed to live, is this one:

> **Honesty with Colleagues:** If you have a problem with a decision or action someone on your team has taken, talk about it with respect. Get it out on the table. Don't let it fester.

And let's assume, too, that another of the organizational values we have both said we want to live is the following:

> **Let People Shine:** Give team members the freedom to come up with their own solutions. There is usually more than one way to get the job done right. Don't pretend yours is the only way.

Now, one day you and I are working on an important project together...and you realize you have a problem with my working style. Specifically, you think I have been micromanaging you, which, as it turns out, I have. By the way, this fact does not make me an *evil* person. And pointing it out does not make you a *good* person. The two of us are just people, learning as we go along. People have blind spots, and micromanaging is one of mine.

So what do you do? You do me the favor of acting in full alignment with the *Honesty with Colleagues* value. You find an appropriate time to talk to me one on one about what you see as this habit I have of micromanaging you. We discuss my habit of telling you exactly *how* to do minute aspects of your job. We agree that you should really have the latitude to figure out how to do certain things on your own, based on your own work history, preferences, and behavioral style. You raise this issue with me and find a respectful way to communicate to me that I have not been aligning with the value *Let People Shine.*

To my credit, I listen, I acknowledge that there is a disconnect with this value on my side, I thank you for the feedback, and I resolve to fix that problem I am creating—fast.

A week after you and I have that conversation, I now have the issue of "micromanaging" on my personal radar screen. In other words, this is truly something I want to change. I am making a special point of looking out for that behavior, because I know that it does not align with the value of *Letting People Shine*, and it is personally important to me that I align with that value. So that week goes by, you and I work together on Project A, and I do not fall back into any behavioral patterns that could even remotely be construed as micromanaging. Then, next week, a big deadline comes our way. You and I get to work together on Project B, which is pretty intense. And without even realizing it, I slip back into micromanaging you. Maybe it is a reaction to how important I think the project is. Maybe I have simply forgotten. It does not matter. The point is, I have lost the value.

At this stage, there are a number of interesting paths we can go down, *only one of which supports and protects the culture.*

The first path is that you simply ignore the fact that I am micromanaging you. You give up on the value of *Honesty with Colleagues* for whatever reason, and you *do not* find an appropriate, respectful way to address what is happening with me. In this case, you and I are *each* failing to protect the culture. I am failing to live the value of *Letting People Shine*, you are failing to live the value of *Honesty with Colleagues*, and neither of us is doing anything about it. So we are not protecting the culture.

The second path is that one of us brings the issue up—with a negative attitude. In other words, we use the fact that there has been a disconnect with the values as a justification for launching some kind of personal attack. We focus not on the behavior, but on the other person. You might do that by saying something like, "I guess you were just kidding when you said you were going to live the value of *Letting People Shine*." I might do that by saying, "Listen, I don't want to hear any static from you about how I'm not living the values. This project is just too important for that. We have to get it right. Period. If I find a detail that needs fixing, I'm going to tell you about it, and we can sort out whatever we need to sort out about the values after we submit Project B." *Either* of those responses is a failure to protect the values and the culture!

The third path we can go down is the one where we work on the front end—together. This is the path where we acknowledge that we are both human beings and both works in progress. Because we are both human, we are both subject to recurring blind spots. In this case, the blind spot is mine. So what I need from you is an appropriate, respectful reminder that I have fallen into the habit of micromanaging. Once you give me that reminder, we can find a way to complete Project B in a way that honors all the company values…*and* supports our relationship as human beings. What you need from me is fulfillment of the commitment to keep the working space safe by responding calmly and without judgment to what you have to say. You need me to accept that the quality of our relationship matters more than the completion of Project B. And you need me to look for ways to do a better job of living the value. When we work on the front end of a values mismatch, we are working on the relationship, which means we are supporting each other's mutual commitment to helping each other grow and develop over time. That is the best possible way to protect the culture. *Work the front end of the relationship, not just the back end where the results show up!*

> **Work the front end of the relationship, not just the back end where the results show up!**

As Ron Mittelstaedt of Waste Connections puts it: "When we are going along and we have somebody that is struggling in some area that impacts the values, we try to work with them proactively. That is our first goal. Obviously, our response depends on the severity of the situation, but first and foremost we are working to proactively counsel them so that they can be the ones who take the lead role in modifying the behavior. Our goal is to help them take the lead in changing it. Maybe it's a one-off instance, maybe it's not. But we want to put the time in on the relationship so that, ideally, they can recognize that this is something that they can change and they are willing to change."

BE SURE TO WORK THE FRONT END!

And by the way, if you remind me of my blind spot about micromanaging (or anything else) and my instant response is, "I don't micromanage you all of the time, just SOME of the time!"—then I am not working the front end. I am not protecting the culture.

Remember: Agreeing to live the value means that *the minute* I lose the value, I acknowledge what happened and find a way to fix the problem—fast! Being committed to the values means *no matter what.*

> "Freedom begins with owning your flaws and disowning your fears."
> —Umair Haque

There is no room for self-justification, no room for excuses for the times in the past when I lost sight of the values. I need to own those. I need to fix the problem. And I need to move on.

VI

Celebrate the
CULTURE

Chapter 18

The Test

THE FIFTH STEP, Celebrate the Values, reveals the true character of the senior leader of the organization. This step reveals whether that leader truly values people *as people.* It is a major test.

Many, many leaders fail this test because most of what they do to celebrate the culture is fundamentally inauthentic. What do I mean by inauthentic? I mean that the "celebration" in question does not connect to the culture and is not rooted in true care, concern, and appreciation for people *as individuals.*

Every little step forward that we take, both individually and as an organization, must be recognized authentically on a person-to-person level…and must be connected back to the culture. When we do that, we are celebrating the culture. When we do not do that, we are celebrating something else. (Probably ourselves.)

> Every little step forward that we take, both individually and as an organization, must be recognized authentically on a person-to-person level…and must be connected back to the culture.

The plaque on the wall, the high five, the party with cake and ice cream at 4:30, or whatever else we are checking off the list—all of these may be a nice enough way to pass the time, but guess what? If the people we are leading do not see and experience a stronger personal relationship with us based on something they have learned, accomplished or, achieved...if they do not experience a deeper personal connection to the organization's unique culture as a result of that connection...then the "celebration" is likely to do more harm than good. Why? Because it is going to be perceived as fake.

And, all too often, it *is* fake. The leader is not really *celebrating* the person who made the step forward. The leader is only going through the motions.

CELEBRATE is a critical step in this process, and it is the one that senior leaders are most likely to miss entirely, imagining that they have fulfilled it. The reason this happens is that consciously or unconsciously, some leaders make the "celebration" all about them.

When an important milestone or achievement comes up, the leader may actually believe that *they* are the reason for the celebration. But they may not always want to say that out loud. So what do they do? They start setting up "celebrations" that convey no personal engagement with the individual or the team. Rather than communicating meaningfully with anyone about something that person has learned, accomplished, or achieved, and then tying that back to the culture, they order cake and ice cream and invite everyone into the break room at 4:30. They do not say anything of substance about the people, collectively or individually, and they do not say anything of substance about the values. That is fake. And people pick up on that fakeness.[3]

---

3   There is a time and a place for large-scale celebrations, of course. We just need to make sure they connect to some specific achievement and fully align with our values and with our relational commitments. Just remember that they do not replace the individual connections we have been discussing and that they often provide good opportunities to celebrate individual achievements and milestones.

Look again at our definition of Celebration: as leaders, *we must find a way to recognize authentically every single step forward that we take, both individually and as an organization…and we must tie that back to the culture.*

You will recall the true story I told you about the Happy State Bank teller who got a call from a customer who was having trouble with her debit card—the teller who made the withdrawal on the customer's behalf and drove the cash over to Walmart so the customer could pay for her groceries. Here is what an authentic celebration of that event might look like during a team meeting. You gather your team together, and you say something like this:

> *Everyone, please give me your attention for a moment. You all know Joan. Yesterday, Joan did something I thought was important and worth noticing, something that really captures one of the values we live by: CUSTOMER SERVICE IS **THE** GOAL. [Here you share the details of what Joan did for the customer who was having trouble with her debit card.] Now, that is **exactly** what that value looks like in action. Can everyone please join me in giving Joan a round of applause for showing us what that value looks like in action? Thank you, Joan. (Applause.)*

Here is what an authentic celebration of that event would *not* look like: During the team meeting, you say:

> *Joan's manager tells me you guys are doing a great job on the customer service front. I just have to tell you, that kind of news really makes my day. Keep it up! I want you to know that I think you guys rock! I appreciate all you do! I've arranged for cake and ice cream in the break room for the whole team. See you there at 4:30!*

This kind of inauthenticity from the senior leader kills a high-performance culture.

Notice that the first message is all about what *Joan* did, and the second message is all about the leader! (Count the "I," "me," and "my" pronouns!)

MEAN IT!

When it comes to celebration, we have to mean what we say. We have to say what really matters, and we have to connect what we say to the culture. Otherwise, all the work we have done in steps one through four will go to waste. Our people will disengage.

There is a basic human need to be noticed, acknowledged, valued, and appreciated. Our job as leaders in step five is to make sure they experience being noticed, acknowledged, valued, and appreciated *for living the culture.* And if we do not do this, we should not delude ourselves that someone else is going to do it. Everyone takes their cues from the person at the top. We set the example…we cannot celebrate the culture authentically unless we are authentically celebrating *PEOPLE LIVING THE CULTURE…*and we cannot do that unless we value them *as individuals.*

Very often, this means acknowledging *failure,* because failure is how human beings learn. Again, we are talking about celebrating *every single step forward.* Whenever someone on our team learns from a failure, whenever someone clearly identifies what *does not* work and gets a little closer to implementing what *does* work, that is a reason to celebrate! That celebration may take place privately on a small scale, or it may take place publicly on a large scale. It may be about something that relates directly to work, or it may be about something that happens in the person's life outside of the organization. But as the leader, *we must know about the step forward, we must find a way to recognize it authentically on a personal level, and we must tie it back to the culture.* So when someone gets better at managing inventory, we find a way to recognize that, because that is a step forward. And when someone's child graduates from college, we find a way to recognize *that,* too, because that is also a step forward! We do not just look for opportunities to authentically celebrate organizational victories. We look for ways to authentically celebrate *every* meaningful victory that takes place in someone's life. And if our knowledge of what is going on in a team member's life is so shallow that we have no idea what their victories outside the organization look like, shame on us.

> We do not just look for opportunities to authentically celebrate organizational victories. We look for ways to authentically celebrate *every* meaningful victory that takes place in someone's life. And if our knowledge of what is going on in a team member's life is so shallow that we have no idea what their victories outside the organization look like, shame on us.

At this stage, I have to remind you about the ten relational commitments we looked at earlier in the book, and about three in particular. Remember that leaders at all high-performance organizations buy into and fulfill all ten of these commitments...and notice how these three specific commitments connect powerfully to the non-negotiable step of CELEBRATE:

I COMMIT TO HELPING INDIVIDUALS REACH THEIR POTENTIAL AND BE THEIR BEST. When your people know you care about their growth and development, they care about the organization's growth and development.

I COMMIT TO EMBRACING FAULTS AND FAILURES AS WELL AS OPPORTUNITIES AND SUCCESSES. Taking on this commitment means taking on the mindset of "I am not perfect, and I do not expect others to be perfect."

I COMMIT TO STANDING WITH YOU WHEN ALL HELL BREAKS LOOSE. Are you there when people need you?

Celebrating the culture always starts with celebrating the people. That is what flips the switch. That is what engages the team. If you truly value people enough to celebrate them *as individuals*, then you as the leader are going to be all in when it comes to fulfilling these three critical relational commitments. Specifically...

- You will always be open to identifying new opportunities for them to grow, thrive, and contribute at a higher level.

- You will always make sure that people know that you do not expect perfection from them every time and that making an innocent mistake, a mistake they can and do learn from, is not going to get them fired.

- You will make absolutely sure they know you will be there for them when they need you.

This is what leaders who truly care about people do. Follow through on these relational commitments as you celebrate people for bringing the culture you have designed, modeled, taught, and protected to life. If you can do that, you will give your organization an unmatchable competitive advantage in the marketplace: a work environment where people are constantly on the lookout for newer and better ways to live and celebrate their high-performance culture. On the other hand, if you *do not* value people enough to make and fulfill these commitments, you cannot expect to complete step five of the Accountability Advantage process, because you will have joined the long list of leaders who failed the test of caring about people *as people*. That is not a list you want to show up on. Passing this test means your team has flipped the switch. They are engaged. They are committed to making good things happen.

> "Turned on people figure out how to beat the competition. Turned off people only complain about being beaten by the competition."
>
> —Ben Simonton

Are you "all in" for passing this test? If so, let's keep going.

Chapter 19

Celebration Delivers "I Love Working Here"

HAVE YOU EVER talked to someone who was absolutely in love with the company they work for? Someone who counted every day as a blessing because they were in a job, and part of a team, that made them look forward to going to work, day after day after day? I have. I see that all the time. This is one of the major advantages of doing what I do for a living. I get to help people take part in the kind of working culture that empowers them to do what they love, for an organization they love, with people they love spending time with. And let me tell you: it is something to behold.

> "Doing what you love is the cornerstone of having abundance in your life."
>
> —Wayne Dyer

The person's eyes light up when they start talking about what they do for a living. They radiate enthusiasm, not just about what they do for a living, but about the mission of the organization. Best of all, they attract talent. They are like a magnet for the best and the brightest who wish they loved *their* jobs…but do not.

Believe it. Someone who is in love with the organization is the most powerful recruiting advertisement imaginable. So, how do we get there? How do we make that happen?

We start by reminding ourselves that whenever someone says, "I love working here," what they are actually saying is "I love working in this culture, and I love working with these people." They do not love the building, or the sign outside the building, or the street where that sign is posted. They love the *people*; they love the daily experience they have of working with those people because of the culture that leadership has designed, modeled, taught, protected, *and* celebrated.

Here is the point: if you skip the last step, the part that connects to authentic appreciation for the human beings who are actually making the effort and actually living the culture, then you never get to "I love working here." Letting people know that you value them personally is what makes "I love working here" happen. It is what sets a powerful example that inspires people at all levels to connect with and celebrate others in the same authentic, personal way.

If leaders set the right example, celebration becomes part of the way the organization does business, and team members celebrate each other's milestones without having to be reminded or encouraged to. On the other hand, if all leaders value is the way someone's contributions connect to some short-term income report or to their own image, then *those leaders do not value the team members as people.* They are means to an end. Any attempts to celebrate them will ring hollow, and they *will not* love working for the organization, because they are in a culture by default.

It never ceases to amaze me how many leaders seem to go out of their way to create the kind of working environment where you cannot possibly imagine any of the team members saying to each other in private, unguarded moments, "Wow, I really love working here." Leaders sabotage their own organizations and make it impossible for team members to feel that way about the culture when they say things like this:

"I know I ride you hard sometimes, but that's how we achieve great things." Notice how this makes it all about the leader. This is manipulative self-aggrandizement, and we have an obligation to stay far away from it.

"Nobody said it was going to be easy. If you don't like it, you don't have to work here." Does that make you feel like recruiting your friends and family? No.

"I shouldn't have to pat you on the back or tell you 'You win' every time you do a good job. If you're a professional, you shouldn't need reinforcement or a high five or any kind of incentive to do a good job. That's what I'm paying you for, isn't it? To do a good job. Your paycheck is your high five." This is a common and particularly cruel variation of the "Nothing personal, it's just business" justification that some leaders pull out when they do not feel like investing time, energy, or attention in their relationships with their own people.

What makes these responses not just ill-conceived, but cruel, is the implication that if the team members were only mature enough, professional enough, or competent enough, they would not *need* any kind of positive emotional connection with the person in charge of their team—or with anyone else. And you know what? That is nonsense. It is the kind of thing an accountable leader never, ever says or (this is crucial) *even thinks* about someone on their team.

As members of the big team known as *humanity*, we are, by definition, all about emotional connections. We are all about getting reinforcement. We notice when someone values us and when someone does not. No one is so good at their job or so professional that they give up their membership in the human race and their need for human connection. Anyone who tells you otherwise is selling you a bill of goods.

If "You shouldn't need a pat on the back" is really how you feel about your relationship with even *one* of your team members, you might as well give this book to someone else. Leaders who are ready to start taking relational commitments seriously simply do not think like that. Nothing I can share with you here will help you learn to celebrate the people and the culture until you set aside the delusion that your relationship with that team member is not rooted in personal appreciation and acknowledgment. To the degree that we attempt to lead via a relationship that ignores the need for authentic, personal celebration of the other person's growth and progress, *that relationship is dysfunctional.*

> To the degree that we attempt to lead via a relationship that ignores the need for authentic personal celebration of the other person's growth and progress, *that relationship is dysfunctional.*

Of course people are supposed to work hard. Of course they are supposed to be competent and perform their work at a high level of proficiency. Of course they are supposed to be focused on delivering excellence. But none of that changes the reality that they are also human beings. Human beings grow and thrive and contribute to the degree that their relationships with others *inspire* them to grow, thrive, and contribute. An accountable leader is going to remember that.

An accountable leader, one who is focused like a laser beam on celebrating the culture, knows there is always a relationship to strengthen, that there is always a connection to make or improve with someone on the team. That kind of leader is always going to be looking for a way to take the relationship to the next level by personally and authentically acknowledging what the person has learned, noticing what they have accomplished, and appreciating them for living the culture. The accountable leader knows that in the final analysis, *the people are the culture.* Such a leader never tires of finding and celebrating, with genuine passion, examples of behavior that show the culture is on track and that the team is putting into practice what they say they believe.

> **The people are the culture.**

Who wants to be part of a culture where the norm is belittling and humiliating people for wanting to connect, for wanting to be valued? Who makes a point of telling their friends, family, and associates how much they love working at an organization like that? Who sticks around at such an organization when the chance to work somewhere else, somewhere they will be truly valued, comes along?

Nobody.

CHANGING HOW WE THINK ABOUT PEOPLE

So here is the big takeaway about celebration: if you are the senior leader in the organization and you are still trapped in the mindset of

"That's what I pay them for," then you cannot expect to fulfill step five, Celebrate the Culture.

What you *can* expect is for people to do the bare minimum for you whenever they hear that kind of thing from you or see that attitude in action. If you want them to go above and beyond the call of duty for you, you must be willing to go above and beyond for them. That means getting yourself and your organization *out* of the "That's what I pay them for" mindset. That means changing the way you think about your people.

Changing the way you think about your people requires that you set your sights on the very best of what is possible in your relationship with them, based on the values you have defined. It requires you to notice whenever the best shows up, and it requires you to express authentic, person-to-person gratitude about what happened, not just once, but repeatedly. This is, for many leaders, a whole new way of life—and a liberating decision.

Now, instead of catching people in the act of making a mistake, you catch them in the act of living the culture you have designed and modeled…and then you show some appreciation! Connect the culture to the successes. That is the only way to get your team to the emotional space that makes the feeling "I love working here!" a daily reality.

> If you are a leader, and especially if you are the senior leader, SHOW SOME AUTHENTIC APPRECIATION when you catch people in the act of living the culture you have designed.

MAKE CULTURE THE DAILY PRIORITY

Instead of trying to convince people that *we* are important, we want to create a unified feeling among all the team members that *the culture* is important. And we do that by making the culture a daily priority.

I know an exceptionally well-qualified attorney—I'll call her Ellen—who left a high-paying job at a prominent law firm because there was something about the culture at that firm that just was not working for her. The daily routine there was, as she described it, "No fun." This is a common description of a culture by default. When the culture is established by default, that means that designing, modeling, teaching, protecting, and celebrating the culture *is not an organizational priority.*

Ellen moved on to a new law firm, one that seemed like a better fit for her. After she completed her very first project, she got a call from her direct supervisor, congratulating her on completing her first assignment and making several remarks that demonstrated her awareness of the quality of Ellen's work. "You did a great job," she told Ellen. "The level of work you did on that project was just outstanding. I'm glad you decided to come here and be part of our team." She wasn't faking it. She had looked closely at Ellen's work. She meant it. She really was proud that Ellen had decided to join them.

That is what celebrating the people and celebrating the culture looks like.

It was in that moment that Ellen realized what had not been working for her at her old job: *no one there had ever said anything positive about her work or even noticed its quality.* No one there cared enough about the relationships to support them by celebrating the people and their contributions and their willingness to live the culture. In fact, no one at the old firm had even bothered to define or model the culture, much less celebrate it! She knew, with deep certainty, that she had made the right career choice.

So lesson one in Ellen's story is: If you want to live and experience a culture that delivers excellence in all its forms, you had better make culture a daily priority—by *celebrating* excellence every time you see it!

Lesson two of Ellen's story is just as important. And the story does not end with that phone call she received from the partner! The most important part of the story, in fact, is still to come.

Ellen told everyone in her immediate circle about that call she got from the partner telling her that she had done an excellent job. She shared that conversation with family, friends, colleagues, you name it. She was so moved, so empowered, so excited by the experience of having her good work noticed and celebrated that she made a point of *sharing that experience with the people who were most important in her life.* Isn't that what we want people to do? Is there any better recruiting and retention policy than having people who love working for our organization *tell other people* how much they love what they do all day long and how much they love the people they do it with? What better strategy could there be for attracting, retaining, and growing the people with the highest potential to contribute?

> If you want to **earn a reputation** as an organization with a culture that delivers excellence in all its forms, then you had better make culture a daily priority—by **celebrating** excellence every time you see it!

NEVER FORGET:
THE PEOPLE ARE THE CULTURE!

Every time we celebrate an individual for doing the right thing, we are also celebrating the culture.

Every time we celebrate a team for doing the right thing, we are also celebrating the culture.

Every time we celebrate someone who is *joining* the team and *agreeing* to do the right thing, we are also celebrating the culture.

Understand: *The culture is the collective totality of the decisions, actions, and choices that human beings make in support of the goal of creating a more accountable organization…and, ultimately, a more accountable world.* These decisions, actions, and choices include, but are not limited to…

- Living and discussing the values we have defined and agreed to live by.

- Living and discussing the ten core relational commitments.

- Defining the culture in unconditional support of those who are not yet familiar with it.

- Modeling the culture on an ongoing basis, as part of who we are and what we do each and every day in this organization, regardless of whether or not we hold a formal leadership position.

- Teaching the culture on an ongoing basis, regardless of whether or not we hold a formal leadership position.

- Protecting the culture on an ongoing basis, regardless of whether or not we hold a formal leadership position (by, for instance, speaking up when we see someone take an action or make a decision that we believe is not in accordance with a stated value).

- Celebrating the culture by finding an appropriate way to acknowledge people who are committed to it, whether or not we hold a formal leadership position. (Yes, you can celebrate someone for celebrating the culture!)

- Spreading the good word about the organization and its mission.

Any time any of these things happens and we connect positively with someone who made it happen, *we are celebrating the culture!* And every time we celebrate the culture, we empower the people in the organization to claim a deeper level of personal ownership of the culture. Only when they live and own the culture on a personal level do they reach the point of "I love working here!"

Recently I spoke with Homam Hashem, director general at Kafalah (part of The Saudi Investment Bank), about how celebrating the culture has played out at his organization. This is what he had to say:

We've been working together for nearly a year now. What kinds of changes have you been seeing?

Certainly, the biggest change is that we are now receiving much more support and acknowledgment from senior government officials than we were before we started working with you on cultural issues. That happens roughly once a week now, Sam, and I believe it is happening because people in government are seeing real progress in terms of what we are accomplishing. So that is certainly very gratifying. And it all connects to what you taught us and helped us to reinforce about developing a high-performance culture, and in particular about Celebration. We catch people in the act of living the values, and we acknowledge that. It has made a difference.

Can you talk a little bit about changes in the relationships among your team members?

Internally, I would say there have been more positive changes than I can count. But one that definitely stands out is that you see team members making much more of an effort to support each other. Teamwork is now one of the key principles at Kafalah; it is part of who we are. Everyone knows now that this is not a one-man show. What we do here is never about a single person. You give something to a team, and you know they will have each other's backs. This is something I am so proud of, and it connects directly to the work we have done with you on accountability. I'll give you an example. During some of our meetings, each individual team member is tasked with presenting specific loan cases to the committee. Of course, some people are better at presenting to groups than others are. Before we started working with you, what would happen would be that some analyst would be having a little trouble presenting his case, and all his colleagues would sit back and watch. Now, something very different happens. The minute someone starts to struggle, a colleague will immediately step up and help him over that rough spot. That is teamwork in action, and it is wonderful to see.

What about changes in the way the employees view Kafalah as an employer?

This has been one of the most remarkable turnarounds. We used to have a situation where people were constantly saying bad things about the organization. That has all changed. Now, employees do not say bad things about Kafalah. It simply does not happen. Employees all start from the point of view that they are part of the organization and they are positive in their outlook and in their expectations. A few years ago, when I would listen in on what people were saying about the organization, most of the time I heard negative comments. Now, every meeting, every social gathering, everyone is positive. People feel that they are very lucky to be part of this team. And so they speak that way and act that way. It has been an extraordinary transformation.

I would also say that since we started working with you on strengthening and celebrating the culture, Sam, it seems to me that the vision and the mission are much more frequent topics of conversation and focus among the members of the team. These subjects just keep appearing everywhere, and I think that is a very positive development. Nowadays, I think people are much more likely to see the culture in action, and discussions about the culture are more likely to be an integral part of how the team socializes. We've learned that Celebration does not have to be an external event. Those events are wonderful, and they are important, but finding ways to celebrate the culture every day, even when you aren't doing something outside of work with the team, is more important. Doing that has helped our people to be more mission-focused and to begin really claiming ownership of projects. It has helped everyone to become a leader, someone who takes the initiative and acts in the best interests of the team and the organization, regardless of whether or not they have been given formal leadership responsibilities. And that was exactly what we wanted.

What kinds of changes have you seen on the management side?

Another change that's happened since we started working with you is that managers are now assigning projects to an entire team. It is not just the manager's name that shows up in the project assignments now. Now we spotlight the team as a whole. The entire team takes ownership of the outcome of the project. This is an essential part of enablement.

In addition, there is a much stronger connection in terms of the leadership's ongoing commitment to the team. After working with you and after senior management has had the chance to see what is possible, there is a much stronger sense, not just at the management level but throughout the organization, of being committed to each other. There is a prevailing attitude of "We cannot let the team down." That was not the situation before we started working with you.

Any final thoughts you'd like to share with leaders?

Yes. When you fix the environment, when you make the culture the priority, that means you must stop fixating on short-term performance metrics. Those are not the priority. Don't worry about the numbers in the short term. The numbers will take care of themselves. That has been our experience. Fix the team, and the team will bring you the numbers. Invest in the training, invest the time, fix the culture, celebrate the culture. I believe you will like the numbers that result.

FIX THE CULTURE!

If I had to pick one and only one takeaway for leaders from Homam Hashem's powerful interview, it would be this one: *Fix the culture, fix the team, and the team will bring you the numbers.* That's a reminder of the tremendous power of accountability—and of celebration.

Chapter 20

Mindset Is the Key to Celebrating the Culture

OFTEN, I AM ASKED to condense the basics of accountable leadership into a single sentence. Here is that sentence: *Accountability is not a way of doing; accountability is a way of thinking.*

Changing your thinking means changing your mindset. Specifically, we need to change our mindset on how we think about people. An Accountable Mindset is absolutely essential for leaders who want to get better at celebrating the high-performance culture they have designed, modeled, taught, and protected. If we are serious about setting the personal standard that encourages *everyone* in the organization to celebrate the culture authentically, then we are going to learn how to take on, return to, and model, an Accountable Mindset—day after day, hour after hour, and minute after minute.

Here are the ten essential facts that leaders—and everyone else— need to know about adopting, and living, an Accountable Mindset:

ONE: *Your mindset is what you believe* about yourself, the world, and other people.

TWO: *Your mindset is always with you.* Even if you think your mindset does not affect your perceptions and decisions, it does.

THREE: *At any given moment, your mindset is either toxic or accountable.* There is no middle ground. It is *always* one or the other, and where you land on that is up to you.

FOUR: *There are three and only three Accountable Mindsets: Gratitude, Abundance, and Respect.* The flip side of each Accountable Mindset is a Toxic Mindset: Entitlement, Scarcity, and Contempt.

FIVE: This means *there are three Mindset Transitions* that accountable people learn to make:

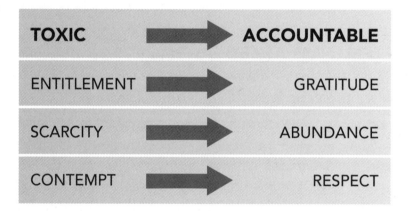

SIX: *People who give up Entitlement so they can live in the Gratitude Mindset never stop looking for opportunities to give.* They know that everyone and everything is connected. That is why they are eager to give the gift of celebrating even seemingly minor cultural victories. They know that even those minor victories eventually touch everyone and lead to major victories! There is something special that happens when you give and give freely. If you operate from the position that you are looking for opportunities to give without remorse, without feeling coerced—if you truly give from your heart—something opens up inside of you and new possibilities present themselves in support of the gratitude you have initiated. This spirit of gratitude is essential for authentic celebration.

SEVEN: *People who give up Scarcity so they can live in the Abundance Mindset learn to see opportunity everywhere* and are endlessly grateful on a personal level for the blessings in their lives. Scarcity is rooted in fear. It produces lack, desperation, and conflict. The Scarcity Mindset, and the unreasoning fear that drives it, can undermine and eventually destroy, not just working relationships, but all relationships. Abundance, by contrast, is rooted in love, gratitude, and possibility. It strengthens and empowers all our relationships, and it lies at the heart of any authentic celebration of the culture.

EIGHT: *People who give up Contempt so they can live in the Respect Mindset accept that every viewpoint matters,* even if it is not one they happen to share. When we consider another human being solely as a means to an end—our end—and we treat them accordingly, we are locked into the Toxic Mindset of Contempt. On the other hand, when we celebrate them authentically for living the culture, we see them as human beings who can grow, learn, and contribute more over time. We stop thinking in the short term. This is an essential prerequisite of true celebration.

NINE: *Choosing to live in an Accountable Mindset always deepens your celebration of the culture,* because this choice supports and deepens your commitment to your relationships. Choosing to live in a Toxic Mindset, by contrast, always undermines your celebration, because this choice degrades your commitment to your relationships.

TEN: *Your mindset is always a matter of choice.* You always have the choice of making it toxic or making it accountable. Many people make this choice unconsciously or semi-consciously and lean toward the toxic. This makes authentic celebration impossible. Accountable people, on the other hand, make the choice of mindset *consciously,* because they are committed to developing themselves and other people to the highest and best level of potential…and they know that a Toxic Mindset is incompatible with that commitment.

Notice that the three Toxic Mindsets are all about *me*…and the three Accountable Mindsets are all about *us*. This is because accountability is ultimately focused on supporting relationships though service.

> The three Toxic Mindsets (Entitlement, Scarcity, and Contempt) are all about *me*…and the three Accountable Mindsets (Gratitude, Abundance, and Respect) are all about *us*.

Notice, too, that when you take on an Accountable Mindset, you apply it to yourself as well as to the people you serve. You too deserve Gratitude. You too deserve Abundance. You too deserve Respect. When you celebrate the culture by taking on these mindsets over and over and over again, you end up raising your own game, not just someone else's game!

> "What you focus on is what multiplies." —Kylie Francis

Why bother with any of this? Why take the trouble of changing the way you think about people and relationships? Because that is what we want team members to do on behalf of customers and others who rely on our organization.

Never forget: Celebrating the culture is equal parts celebrating your values and celebrating your people. At the end of the day, you are celebrating both!

> Never forget: Celebrating the culture is equal parts celebrating your values and celebrating your people. At the end of the day, you are celebrating both!

The CELEBRATE step is all about making sure that the internal experience of the working culture is everything it should be. It is hard to overstate how important that is. Our customers, our clients, all the external people we want to be sure have a great experience cannot get a great experience if the people inside our organization are getting a lousy experience.

> The experience external people have with our organization can never exceed the quality of the experience our internal people have.

The experience external people have with our organization can never exceed the quality of the experience our internal people have. To create a quality internal experience, we master the CELEBRATE step. We learn how to return again and again to an Accountable Mindset.

We make sure the people on the inside feel valued, and cared for, and included, and yes, loved. Only when we do these things are our people empowered to deliver that same kind of experience to the people who operate outside the organization.

Now Is All You Ever Have

WHEN I FIRST STARTED thinking about the best way to begin the final chapter of this book, I found myself drawn to the powerful words of the great author and teacher Eckhart Tolle. Tolle shared an observation that has stood out for me since I first came across it. Here it is:

> "Now is all you ever have. There never is anything else. So you might as well make the now your friend. Otherwise you are out of alignment with life itself."
> —Eckhart Tolle

This quote is apt for leaders and organizations aspiring to secure the Accountability Advantage™ because there is an unfortunate tendency to relegate working on the culture to that long list of important things we mean to get around to eventually. This is a fundamental misunderstanding. Our working culture—and indeed, our whole life—is defined by our response to what is happening *right now*. This instant that is right in front of us is all we ever have to work with and all we ever will have. We are either using this moment to fulfill the values and keep our relational commitments, or we are not. There is no "eventually." There is no "when we have time." There is no "when we make more money." There is no "later." This is it.

Whether we are the senior leader or the most recent hire, whether our organization operates in the for-profit realm or the nonprofit world, whether our team is big or small, whether we are operating locally or globally, whether we are brand new or we have been around forever, we have only this moment to win others to the way of thinking about people that I have outlined in this book: *accountable thinking*. In this moment, the moment staring us in the face *right now*, there are three things that we can count on to attract people to our cause:

We can use the moment before us to project full **confidence** *in the power of authentic human connection to overcome any obstacle.* It is right to be confident in this way, because human connection is, at the end of the day, the only real resource any organization has—and it can and does work wonders.

We can use the present moment to deliver full **transparency** *in our interactions with those with whom we are lucky enough to work.* It is right to be transparent with them about anything and everything that affects their interests, as long as that transparency respects the rights of others. And it is right to be transparent about what we do not know and have not yet been able to do.

We can use the moment we are living right now to share our own **faith** *in our purpose (the reason we are here) and in our mission (the action that supports that purpose).* Faith is what kindles hope. Faith is what draws resources to us. If we do not yet have full faith in our purpose and our mission, we need to discover our purpose and create a compelling mission that puts that purpose into action.

Those are the three things that attract people to a cause: *confidence, transparency,* and *faith.*

When I think of the people who have made a huge difference in my life—the people who emerged as important role models for me; the people I wanted to work with, learn more from, and develop a deeper relationship with—I always find that what made me want to connect with them was the fact that they consistently lived these three things: *confidence, transparency,* and *faith.*

They always had confidence in how they handled themselves, in the way they made decisions, and in what they believed. They were always transparent; they were not afraid to be vulnerable, and they were not afraid to admit their mistakes. In being transparent, they shared their humanness with me, which I found compelling, because they were showing me how they were human, rather than how they were perfect. And they always had full faith in their own values. I could tell that there were certain things that were important to them, things that drove them, things they were unwilling to compromise on and would take a stand for. One of those things, inevitably, was that they believed in their people. That made me want to connect with them and stay connected with them, because when I'm around someone who believes in their people, I know they believe in me.

To this day, those people still inspire *me* to live that same way— with confidence, transparency, and faith—through the power of their personal example.

Leaders who want to make the Accountability Advantage™ a reality at all levels of their organization face a challenge: they must be sure that all three of these things show up, moment after moment, in service of others and in support of a truly accountable working culture, *starting right now.*

If we can do that, then we are true leaders of the organization, and leaders in life, no matter what formal title we have. And if we are serious about creating and sustaining a high-performance culture, the kind of culture that people want to be a part of, we need to inspire *everyone* to step up as that kind of leader: confident, transparent, and faithful.

The strategies I have shared in this book are meant for everyone, not just for leaders. These strategies have been proven effective at empowering us to build something special, something that serves others, something of deep value, something bigger than ourselves that can outlast us and serve as our legacy: an enduring culture of possibility and accountability. Creating and defending this kind of culture gives us the opportunity to serve others in a way that aligns with our deepest beliefs and brings us joy. This is why we define, model, teach, protect, and celebrate a high-performance culture: to serve others. If we are doing it for any other reason, the culture will not endure. It will not bring joy to anyone. And it will have no lasting impact.

So here is my question for you: Who is your personal role model when it comes to the three traits that will allow you to inspire others and serve others effectively? Whose example will you follow?

Who has been the most influential person in your life? Who has impacted your life in a positive way and made you eager to learn more from them, interact more with them, be more like them? Who has truly been an inspiration to you? Who made you feel good every time you were around them?

I believe we all know and have been touched by at least one person who fits this description. Once you know who yours is, I want you to look very closely at the example that person set for you. I am willing to bet that when you examine their impact on your life, you will find that *confidence*, *transparency*, and *faith* showed up in that special person's relationship with you.

My challenge to you now is to follow their example. Make their past example your present-tense destination. Incorporate those three powerful attributes they lived by—confidence, transparency, and faith—and make them the direction toward which you commit *your* life, day after day, hour after hour, minute after minute, second after second. Start now. That is the real challenge we each face: to live that example in the present moment, the only moment that matters.

If we as leaders can meet that challenge, then I believe we can, as Tolle suggests, make friends with the now, align ourselves with our own lives, and begin tapping into possibilities yet undreamed of. We can live in, and be made more alive by, an accountable culture that is deeply rooted in service, a culture that yields not just positive results, but joy. And that is what I wish for everyone.

About the Author

SAM SILVERSTEIN is founder and CEO of The Accountability Institute™ and the creator of the Certified Accountability Advisor™ designation. Sam's mission is to build a more accountable world. He is the author of numerous books, including *No More Excuses, Non-Negotiable, No Matter What, The Success Model, Making Accountable Decisions, The Lost Commandments, I Am Accountable,* and *The Theory of Accountability.* Sam speaks internationally and works with teams from companies, government agencies, communities, and organizations both big and small to build workplace cultures that inspire and prioritize accountability. His clients include PetSmart, Kraft Foods, Pfizer, the United States Air Force, and United Way. Sam is the past president of the National Speakers Association and has been inducted into the Speakers Hall of Fame.

Book Sam Silverstein
To Speak At Your Next Event

Contact Us

Sam Silverstein, Incorporated
121 Bellington Lane
St. Louis, Missouri 63141
info@SamSilverstein.com
(314) 878-9252

To Order More Copies of
The Accountability Advantage

www.samsilverstein.com

Follow Sam

www.twitter.com/samsilverstein

www.youtube.com/samsilverstein

www.linkedin.com/in/samsilverstein

www.instagram.com/samsilverstein

www.facebook.com/silversteinsam

No More Excuses | Making Accountable Decisions | The Success Model | I Am Accountable

OTHER BOOKS BY
SAM SILVERSTEIN
AVAILABLE EVERYWHERE
BOOKS ARE SOLD or
www.SamSilverstein.com

The Accountability Circle

No Matter What | The Lost Commandments | Non Negotiable | Pivot!